OFFICIAL WORKBOOK:
Read People Like a Book

Patrick King at
PatrickKingConsulting.com

Table of Contents

Introduction

Have you ever met someone in your life who is just so damn good at reading other people? They have this superpower of knowing what is on people's minds, and they can even predict how they will behave just by looking at them.

You may have observed that these people are either good communicators or accurate human lie detectors. In fact, these people have an amazing ability to understand how someone else's mind works, often better than they understand their own.

The good news is that you no longer have to be envious, because this superpower is teachable. You don't need to be a psychiatric expert or an FBI agent to be skilled at people-reading.

Learning to read and understand other people is a talent that may open many doors. People are an integral part of our daily lives, and we rely on their company and cooperation for the fulfillment and peace we seek. The ability to rapidly and precisely assess a person's personality, actions, and hidden motivations improves our ability to connect with them and, ultimately, to achieve what we want from them.

We may adjust our expression to boost persuasion and influence and become more conscious of how we are persuaded or misled. We can also better understand those who are extremely different from us and have different values. Having the ability to read people is invaluable, whether you're rummaging through someone's Facebook profile, interviewing job candidates, or figuring out if a salesman isn't lying about the product they're selling.

It's mind-boggling to consider that everyone you meet will remain mostly unknown to you. And how can we be sure that we know what they are thinking? What do they feel, think, or plan? How can we know what they intend by their actions, what drives them, or how they even see us?

In the following chapters, you will learn to read people by understanding them using various models. By the end of this workbook, you will have a new point of view that will help you accurately read people.

But before we begin, let's talk about YOU first:

On a scale of 1 to 10, evaluate your own people-reading skills. Do you think that you can read people accurately? What makes you think that?

_____

_____

_____

_____

_____

_____

_____

_____

_____

_____

_____

_____

_____

_____

_____

_____

_____

_____

_____

How do you usually "read" people? Describe your process and be as detailed as possible. Do you "get" them in just one look? Do you talk to them to understand them? Or is it a mix of both?

_____
_____
_____
_____
_____
_____
_____
_____

Give us the top three signs that you look for when trying to read someone.

_____
_____
_____
_____
_____
_____
_____
_____
_____
_____
_____
_____

If there is something that you want to improve regarding your people-reading skills, what is it? And where do you think you might be going wrong?

_____

_____

_____

_____

_____

_____

_____

_____

What do you want to gain from reading this book that you will be able to immediately put into practice in your everyday life?

_____

_____

_____

_____

_____

_____

_____

_____

CHAPTER 1: Motivation as a Behavioral Predictor

Think back to a time when you were desperate to "get" someone. It might have been because you cared a lot about how they would act or because you were trying to figure out why they had already acted the way they did.

To figure out why people act the way they do, we have to look at their **motivations**. Humans do things for different reasons. You wouldn't drink water if you weren't thirsty, would you? Whether it's good or bad, conscious or unconscious, there is always something that drives someone to act a certain way. When reading people's behavior, the key is to be aware of their motivations. You have to be aware of what fuels their fire. Why do they do *this*? Why do they do *that*?

As discussed in the book, motivation can be conscious or unconscious. It can even be influenced by psychological, social, financial, and even biological and evolutionary factors, all of which could interact with one another in interesting ways. As a result, motivation varies from person to person.

Imagine two people who are studying for a test. You might think that they just want one thing: to pass the test. Of course, that's a given. But what could be driving that goal?

Person A doesn't care much about their academic performance. But two weeks before the test, his girlfriend dumped him. Instead of barhopping to meet someone new, he chooses to channel his focus and energy into something productive: studying for the test.

Person B, on the other hand, suffers from extreme anxiety. He hates the idea of failing and would do everything to prevent it. The memory of his parents' humiliation when he got a D on a paper as a child motivates him to act in this way. Since then, he has made it a point to prepare well for every test he takes so that he doesn't have to go through the agony of failing again.

If we analyze the examples, Person A's motivation is to protect himself by putting up a defensive wall. He puts "studying" between him and the heartbreak he should be feeling. Meanwhile, Person B is intentionally avoiding the pain of failing because of what happened to him before. In his mind, he is sure that studying for the test will save him from humiliation.

Here is where it helps to be able to read people. The point is, if you know what's actually motivating Person A's behavior, you may be able to ask him to speak about his sadness so that he can deal with it healthily by doing so. Conversely, you wouldn't automatically assume the worst of Person B for declining your pre-exam party invitation if you knew that he was afraid of disappointing his parents.

In this chapter of the workbook, you'll learn how to accurately dissect people's motivations. Are they driven by desire, hate, like and dislike, pleasure and pain, fear, obligation, habit, or force? Once you understand someone's driving forces, you'll be better able to accept their actions as a rational and consistent reflection of who they are as a person.

Their acts may serve as windows into their intentions and, ultimately, their personalities.

Before we train that people-reading muscle, let's see what you think about motivation:

Recall a time when your own motivations highly influenced your behavior, and then a time where it happened to one of your friends. What happened?

_____
_____
_____
_____
_____
_____
_____
_____
_____
_____
_____
_____
_____
_____
_____
_____
_____
_____
_____
_____
_____
_____
_____

Think of one particular person that you would like to know more. What did they do lately that caught your attention? Do you think it's a result of a life circumstance, or is it just the person's personality? What could they be thinking before doing that behavior?

_____

_____

_____

_____

_____

_____

_____

_____

_____

_____

_____

_____

_____

_____

_____

_____

_____

_____

_____

_____

If someone works non-stop because they want to provide for their family and their sibling's family, do you think that their actions are admirable or intriguing? What do you think their motivation is behind those actions?

_____
_____
_____
_____
_____
_____
_____
_____

When you thought of that person's possible motivation behind their behavior, did it change how you look at them? Do you feel enlightened or confused?

_____
_____
_____
_____
_____
_____
_____
_____

How can knowing someone's motivation help you read them better?

_____

_____

_____

_____

_____

_____

_____

_____

Motivation as an Expression of the Shadow

To truly know people's motivations, we must speak to _all of them._ Yes, that includes the parts that we cannot visibly see, their shadow, or what is known as their "dark side."

According to Swiss psychologist Carl Jung, the shadow consists of everything in ourselves that we'd rather not look at. They are the parts of ourselves that we conceal from both others and ourselves. Humans have a hard time seeing their flaws because of emotions like fear, panic, rage, and arrogance.

Shadows are interesting because they continue to exist even when they are not at the forefront of our minds. In reality, they may reveal themselves in less obvious ways, such as via actions, ideas, and emotions, or by showing themselves in nightmares or unexpected lapses of self-control. If we take the time to notice and interpret these traits in other people, we may understand and interact with them better.

Learning about someone else's shadow might be as simple as seeing how it affects your own. If you take offense instead of laughing it off when someone labels you "dumb," then there must be some secret part of you that doesn't want to feel inferior. But the truth is that they are usually projecting when they attack you. They give everyone else the same name that they give themselves. If you keep an eye out for such cues, you may learn to avoid taking things personally and to steer the discussion away from a potentially uncomfortable path.

Before we use this to explore a person's drive to behave the way they do, let's see how aware you are of your own drive:

On a scale of 1 to 10, how much do you recognize your own shadow or "dark side"? What aspect of yourself are you hiding from others?

_____

_____

_____

_____

_____

_____

_____

_____

Is there a time when your shadow manifested itself in your social interactions? What happened between you and those you were interacting with whenever your shadow showed up?

_____

_____

_____

_____

_____

_____

_____

_____

If you are 100 percent aware of your own shadow, what do you think will change in the way you interact with others?

_____

_____

_____

_____

_____

_____

_____

_____

_____

Think of a person you recently clashed with. How can you describe them in terms of personality? How do they present themselves to you and other people?

_____

_____

_____

_____

_____

_____

_____

_____

What do you think is a shadow or "dark side" they don't want to disclose about themselves while they interact with others? How do they overcompensate for that part of themselves that they are hiding?

_____

_____

_____

_____

_____

_____

_____

_____

When you had a disagreement with this person, do you think that their shadow showed up? How did it manifest itself? Do you feel as if they were projecting something onto you?

_____

_____

_____

_____

_____

_____

_____

_____

During the argument, what did they say that really triggered you, and how did you react to it? Do you think that your shadow showed up in this reaction? Why or why not?

_____
_____
_____
_____
_____
_____
_____
_____

If you feel that someone is projecting their shadow onto you, what will you do to show your understanding and compassion to them? How will you turn the argument into a peaceful discussion?

_____
_____
_____
_____
_____
_____
_____
_____

How can you be more aware of someone's "dark side"? What will you look out for when having a conversation with someone?

_____

_____

_____

_____

_____

_____

_____

_____

Our Inner Child Still Lives

Recognizing people's "inner child" is another way to understand their deepest motives. The inner child is our unconscious self that embodies our childhood. Sjöblom and colleagues observed in 2016 that adults' inner children are constantly present. They believed the inner child helps adults order their lives via early childhood experiences and ideas.

How can we better understand individuals by using the philosophy of the inner child? We can tell when someone is acting from their shadow, but we can also tell when someone is being driven by their inner child. For instance, if your spouse is furious and defensive during an argument, it may help you if you understand the behavior as that of a terrified toddler having a tantrum.

If you find yourself acting like a parent, it's likely that the other person is completely associated with their inner child. It is required of us as adults to act responsibly, regulate our impulses, and treat others with decency and consideration. In contrast, a person in "kid mode" may really be a child on some level, compelling you to act like a parent would—by calming, correcting, or shouldering responsibility for the individual.

When you know that someone is acting based on their inner child, it's easier for you to refrain from being a "parent" to them. And the best part is that you can inspire them to become the "adult" they should be.

Now, let's try to understand someone's actions through their inner child.

Is there a person in your life who seems to have "disproportionate emotion," meaning they suddenly become angry, hurt, defensive, or offended?

_____
_____
_____
_____
_____
_____
_____
_____

When they display such emotions, what do you think their inner child looks or behaves like? Is the behavior coming from a spoiled, rebellious, or manipulative child? What do you think they lacked or wanted more of as a child?

_____
_____
_____
_____
_____
_____
_____
_____

When you encounter people who behave like their inner child, how do you usually respond? Do you find yourself taking responsibility for them as if you're their "parent"? Or do you consistently treat them as adults despite their childish acts?

_____
_____
_____
_____
_____
_____
_____

If your friend suddenly pouts and throws a tantrum after you called them out for being rude to the waiter, what do you think their inner child is like? How will you approach the situation without making yourself feel like their "parent"?

_____
_____
_____
_____
_____
_____
_____
_____

Do you think that being aware of someone's inner child can help understand the cause of their behavior? Why or why not?

_____
_____
_____
_____
_____
_____
_____
_____

How can you be keener in spotting someone's inner child? What have you learned in this section that you will definitely use in reading people?

_____
_____
_____
_____
_____
_____
_____
_____
_____

The Motivation Factor—Pleasure or Pain

The pleasure principle is perhaps the best-known theory put forth to explain human motivation. Its widespread popularity stems from the fact that it is also the most straightforward. Researchers as far back as Aristotle in ancient Greece saw how easily people could be controlled and driven by pleasure and pain, but it was Sigmund Freud who popularized the pleasure principle.

The pleasure principle simply states that people actively seek out pleasure and try to avoid pain. This alone can help you predict people's behavior.

As mentioned in the book, there are a few rules governing this principle:

- *Every decision we make is based on gaining pleasure or avoiding pain.*
- *People work harder to avoid pain than they do to experience pleasure.*
- *Perceptions of pleasure and pain are more powerful motivators than actual events.*
- *Survival overrides everything.*

In this part of the workbook, let's see how the pleasure principle plays out in motivating our and other people's actions:

Assess your own and other people's behavior. Do you agree that you are driven to do things because you seek pleasure and avoid pain? Why or why not?

_____

_____

_____

_____

_____

_____

_____

_____

_____

_____

_____

_____

_____

_____

_____

_____

Think of examples for yourself and others. List some scenarios in which you or others are driven to seek pleasure and avoid pain.

_____
_____
_____
_____
_____
_____
_____
_____

Think of someone you want to read. Describe that person's usual actions. If that person is avoiding a kind of pain, what would it be?

_____
_____
_____
_____
_____
_____
_____
_____

If that same person is trying to gain a kind of pleasure, what would it be?

_____
_____
_____
_____
_____
_____
_____
_____

How can you tell whether someone is behaving to avoid pain or to achieve pleasure? How can this help you predict other people's behaviors?

_____
_____
_____
_____
_____
_____
_____
_____
_____
_____
_____
_____

The Pyramid of Needs

In the 1940s, a professor of psychology named Abraham Maslow proposed a new idea: that people are the result of a set of fundamental human needs, the deprivation of which is the major cause of most psychological disorders. As a company, our daily goals revolve around satisfying these requirements.

A hierarchy depicting the development of fundamental human wants and aspirations has been named after Maslow. It's a ladder: If you can't climb it while also satisfying your most fundamental human wants and aspirations, you'll be under a lot of stress and never really feel fulfilled. What this implies is that your reasons for doing anything will vary according to your position in the hierarchy.

If you look at the levels of Maslow's hierarchy of needs, you can tell where you are in terms of what motivates you.

The first stage is physiological fulfillment. Of course, when you're on stage, you need to behave in order to survive.

The second stage is safety. If one's basic needs are met, such as food, clothing, and shelter, then one must devise a plan to assure that these needs will continue to be met.

The third stage is love and belonging. Now that you know you will make it through, you may realize how hollow life may be if you don't have somebody to share it with.

The fourth stage is self-esteem. After securing relationships, you must ensure they are healthy ones that will make you feel confident and supported.

The final stage is self-actualization. Self-actualization, the pinnacle of Maslow's hierarchy, comes last. That's when you are motivated to do something in life that has meaning beyond satisfying your immediate needs.

Although Maslow's theory may fall short of describing our minute-to-minute wants and needs, it does serve as a useful checklist for the big picture of what it is that we want. By keeping an eye on individuals, we may learn about their life stages, present priorities, and needs in order to help them progress.

Evaluate your own behavior recently. Using Maslow's hierarchy of needs, which stage are you fulfilling right now?

_____
_____
_____
_____
_____
_____
_____
_____

Identify the stage that motivates each behavior, and describe how you would react if you encountered such a person:

If a homeless person steals your coffee while you're working at a coffee shop, what could be motivating their stealing behavior?

_____
_____
_____
_____
_____
_____
_____
_____

If your friend, who is a businessman, tries to convince you to go to a spiritual camp, what could be motivating them to invite you?

_____

_____

_____

_____

_____

_____

_____

_____

If your sister, who just became unemployed, yells at you for not helping her look for a job, what do you think is the motivation behind her yelling?

_____

_____

_____

_____

_____

_____

_____

_____

_____

_____

If your divorced mom seeks your comfort as she cries from another breakup, what do you think is motivating her to do this?

_____
_____
_____
_____
_____
_____
_____
_____

If your friend gets upset when no one claps for him during his presentation, what do you think is pushing him to be upset?

_____
_____
_____
_____
_____
_____
_____
_____
_____
_____
_____

If you encounter someone who is stuck on a certain stage, what are your steps to help them move up?

_____

_____

_____

_____

_____

_____

_____

_____

How can you determine someone's stage in the hierarchy of needs? What questions will you ask to know this information? What other things will you observe?

_____

_____

_____

_____

_____

_____

_____

_____

_____

_____

Defense of the Ego

For many of us, the motivation behind our actions is to shelter the ego from potential harm, and there are many good reasons to do so. The ego's natural defense mechanism may distort reality and lead to widespread dishonesty and deceit. Therefore, this is another reliable technique for reading people accurately.

Our egos, pride, and self-esteem are all protected by a variety of well-crafted defense systems. In times of hardship, we may remain whole thanks to these practices. The late Sigmund Freud may be credited with coining the word.

You can learn a lot about why individuals do what they do by studying these so-called defensive mechanisms, which are also excellent predictors of behavior. While everyone's defense systems are unique and interesting in their own way, there are a few consistent themes that you'll notice in other people (and yourself, too!). When the ego is faced with information it disagrees with, fears, or wants to be false, these mental barriers pop up.

To refresh your memory, below are the common defense mechanisms listed in the book. Study them carefully and use them to identify the behaviors in our next activity:

Denial

It's pretty self-explanatory. The perfect example of denial is when someone dies and you refuse to accept that it happened.

Rationalization

The practice of coming up with justifications. Although the undesirable action or fact still stands, it is now framed as something beyond your control and hence unavoidable. A student who did not study for an exam may try to rationalize their poor performance by placing blame on the teacher.

Repression

They have pushed the idea or emotion so far from their mind that they have "forgotten" about it. The dangerous feeling just disappears as if it were never there.

An abused child is one such example. They could want to forget the abuse altogether so they never have to face the agony, especially if they felt unable to prevent it.

Displacement

It entails projecting one's own unpleasant emotions onto something else.

For example, a woman who is tired at work might kick her door before she enters her house just to release the tension.

Projection

Instead of acknowledging that these sentiments belong to us, we project them onto other sources. We fail to acknowledge our own "evil side," instead perceiving it in the behavior of others and laying the blame there.

The perfect example of this is when an unfaithful man accuses his faithful wife of cheating. He feels ashamed of his improper activities, but instead of taking responsibility for them, he blames his partner and becomes suspicious of her motives.

Reaction Formation

The unconscious process through which one counteracts an unpleasant or anxiety-inducing desire by expressing its polar opposite in an extreme or flashy manner. A lady may be horrified by her recent cancer diagnosis, but instead of admitting her anxiety, she may put on a brave front and preach to others that death is nothing to be feared.

Regression

A protective strategy wherein an individual regresses to a more primitive state. This often occurs at times of high tension. For example, a stressed working adult suddenly throws a tantrum and pouts at his boss.

Sublimation

A strategy for self-protection that entails diverting potentially destructive emotions and impulses into more acceptable or useful activities. Like, an upset woman cleans her house instead of acting aggressively.

Think about how you've been acting lately. Which of these defense mechanisms is usually the reason behind your actions?

_____
_____
_____
_____
_____
_____
_____
_____
_____
_____
_____
_____
_____
_____
_____

Observe your recent interactions with people. Which of the defense mechanisms listed above do you believe are the most common? Which do you think are the least?

_____
_____
_____
_____
_____
_____
_____
_____

If an employee justifies their bad performance by blaming their boss's poor leadership skills, which defense mechanism do you think they are using? If you were their boss, how would you approach them?

_____
_____
_____
_____
_____
_____
_____
_____

If someone suddenly craves cotton candy and chocolates when they are stressed from a breakup, which defense mechanism do you think they are using? If you were their friend, how would you help them manage their stress?

_____
_____
_____
_____
_____
_____
_____
_____

Do you think that knowing someone's defense mechanisms will help predict their behavior? Why or why not?

_____
_____
_____
_____
_____
_____
_____
_____
_____
_____

How can you verify someone's coping mechanism? And how will you use that knowledge to understand people more?

_____
_____
_____
_____
_____
_____
_____
_____

Takeaways

- There are a few popular, fairly universal models of motivation that can help you understand people. When you know what drives people, you can see how everything leads back to that, directly or indirectly.
- Seeing the "inner child" in an individual is another strategy for getting to the bottom of people's motivations. The inner child is the part of our psyche that still feels connected to our formative years. In 2016, Sjöblom and colleagues noticed that people's "inner children" never

left them. They reasoned that the experiences and ideas people had as children may help them organize their lives as adults. When we know that someone is acting through their inner child, we can be conscious of not reinforcing those behaviors by refraining from taking a "parent" position.

- The pleasure principle, which asserts that people are naturally inclined to seek out pleasure and avoid suffering, is an excellent place to start when discussing what motivates people. If you stop to consider it, this is all around you, in both little and large ways, every day. Consequently, this makes persons more easily comprehensible. What are individuals hoping to gain, and what are they hoping to avoid? A trace of it persists at all times.

- Abraham Maslow's hierarchy of needs (or the pyramid of needs) explains that as we go through life, our requirements change, and so must our pursuits. By keeping tabs on the stage that other people are on, you may get insight into what drives them. Physiological needs are at the bottom of the hierarchy, followed by safety, then a sense of love and belonging, then pride in oneself, and last, the ability to fully express oneself. Similar to the following paradigm, this one is motivated by the pursuit of satisfaction.

- Ego defense is one of our strongest motivations, yet one that operates mostly below the conscious level. Putting it simply, we take action to protect our ego from anything that can cause us to feel emotionally or mentally diminished. It is so effective at this that we may manipulate reality and tell fibs to ourselves and others without even realizing it. Denial, rationalization, projection, sublimation, regression, displacement, suppression, and response formation are all examples of defense mechanisms that help us avoid taking on or experiencing the effects of responsibilities or unpleasant emotions. When the ego is involved, it usually takes center stage and obscures all other considerations.

CHAPTER 2: The Body, the Face, and Clusters

It's comforting to think that people will eventually show their true colors. While words may be freely exchanged, it has always been understood that actions speak louder than words and that a person's facial expressions or body language may unintentionally reveal their innermost thoughts and feelings. Even though only a small percentage of our communication is verbal, we are constantly sending out signals about our thoughts and emotions.

To most of us, reading people means keeping a close eye on their actions and behaviors as they unfold in the here and now. As intuitive as it may be to assume that where one's body is in space can provide some insight into one's mental state, there is little to no empirical evidence to support this assumption. Even when people make an effort to hide their emotions, motivations, and fears, you can often get a good sense of what they're really like just by looking at them. That said, we can say that the physical cues don't lie.

In the book, it is discussed that decoding facial expressions, body language, and clusters of behavior is not a surefire method of figuring out people. It's important to be careful about making assumptions when interacting with other people and trying to figure out what motivates them. Each of us is unique, and it is essential to consider the larger picture. While there are many tools to decipher nonverbal cues, it's important to keep in mind that no single piece of data can be used to "prove" anything, and that the trick to reading people this way is to keep the big picture in mind as the situation unfolds.

Before we train your skills in reading nonverbal cues, let's assess your current knowledge.

How much do you observe facial expressions and body language? Do you think that they are accurate in revealing something about a person?

_____

_____

_____

_____

_____

_____

_____

_____

When observing someone, what are the first things that you notice, and how do they compare to what you've learned in the book so far?

_____

_____

_____

_____

_____

_____

_____

_____

_____

_____

_____

If a person keeps their arms crossed and cannot sustain eye contact as you interact with them, how would you interpret it? What kind of person are they?

_____

_____

_____

_____

_____

_____

_____

_____

If a person has an open posture, uses their hands when they talk, and looks directly at you when they're speaking, what do you think of them? What kind of personality do they have?

_____

_____

_____

_____

_____

_____

_____

_____

_____

_____

On a scale of 1 to 10, how would you rate yourself when it comes to reading nonverbal cues? Is there something specific that you would like to improve?

_____
_____
_____
_____
_____
_____
_____

What are you looking forward to learning about facial expressions, body language, and behavior clusters that you can apply in reading people?

_____
_____
_____
_____
_____
_____
_____
_____
_____
_____
_____

Look at My Face

In the book, you learned about "macroexpressions" and "microexpressions." To refresh your memory, here is the difference between the two:

"Macroexpressions" are big, obvious, and intense looks on the face that are hard to hide. They are also known as the long-lasting facial expressions because they usually last up to four seconds. "Microexpressions," on the other hand, are instantaneous facial expressions that last for a few hundredths of a second at most. They are usually too brief for the untrained observer to pick up on, but they can reveal a person's innermost feelings and thoughts.

We're all well-versed in decoding "macroexpressions," but catching those "microexpressions" require practice. According to Paul Ekman, expressions on the face are in fact physiological responses. Even when no one is around to see it, you still feel these expressions. He discovered that people of all cultures, even when they were trying to hide their emotions or weren't aware of what they were feeling, still used facial microexpressions in very consistent ways.

Based on his findings, he concluded that everyone, regardless of upbringing, background, or cultural expectation, is capable of making spontaneous, tiny contractions of certain muscle groups that are predictably related to emotions. One thirtieth of a second is the quickest time possible for them.

By being aware of them and learning their meaning, you can get to the heart of what people are really thinking and feeling beneath the surface of what they say. Microexpressions are thought to be more genuine, difficult to fake, or indicative of concealed or rapidly changing emotions than their larger counterparts, macroexpressions, which can be somewhat forced or exaggerated.

Example of a microexpression:

Happiness

- Raised cheeks and mouth corners
- Wrinkles appear around the eyes, under the eyes, and between the upper lip and nose.

Sadness

- The corners of the lips and outer corners of the eyes droop
- Lower lip trembling is possible
- Eyebrows can form a triangle.

Anger

- Eyebrows lower and tense, often downward
- Eyes tighten and lips may purse or open stiffly and penetrate

Fear

- Similar contractions as anger but upward
- The mouth and eyelids are tense whether open or closed.

Surprise

- Shock or surprise will cause rounded, not triangular, brows
- The eyes open wide as the upper and lower eyelids lift and stretch
- Occasionally, the jaw hangs open

Catching those fleeting expressions are tricky, but that's why we're here to boost your skill. Let's put what you learned into practice:

Evaluate how you read facial expressions. Which do you tend to notice more: macroexpressions or microexpressions? Why do you think so?

_____
_____
_____
_____
_____
_____
_____
_____

Look in the mirror. Do each of these emotions and notice what happens in your eyebrows, wrinkles, nose, eyelids, cheeks, mouth, etc. Write your observed microexpressions below.

Happiness

_____

_____

_____

_____

_____

_____

_____

_____

_____

Sadness

_____

_____

_____

_____

_____

_____

_____

_____

Anger

_____
_____
_____
_____
_____
_____
_____
_____
_____
_____

Fear

_____
_____
_____
_____
_____
_____
_____
_____
_____
_____

Disgust

_____

_____

_____

_____

_____

_____

_____

_____

_____

_____

_____

Hate

_____

_____

_____

_____

_____

_____

_____

_____

_____

_____

_____

_____

While you are doing the activity, do you find it easy to portray the emotions? What do you think about your own microexpressions? Do you think that they are hard to fake?

_____
_____
_____
_____
_____
_____
_____
_____
_____
_____
_____
_____
_____
_____
_____
_____
_____
_____
_____
_____
_____
_____

Imagine you are talking to a colleague about a project that he forgot to submit. As you greet him, his mouth is open and his eyebrows are raised. When you start to mention his delayed project, he suddenly raises a side of his mouth. If his face has these microexpressions, what do you think he could be feeling and thinking?

_____
_____
_____
_____
_____
_____
_____
_____
_____
_____
_____
_____
_____
_____
_____
_____
_____
_____
_____
_____

If someone is lying to you, what would their microexpression look like? Describe how you picture their brows, eyes, nose, cheeks, and mouth.

_____

_____

_____

_____

_____

_____

_____

_____

If someone is hiding their anger after feeling offended by someone's rude comment, what would their microexpression look like? Draw it in the box below:

Based on what you learned, how do you plan to practice reading your microexpression-detecting skills? Which microexpression do you find easy to read? Which one is difficult?

_____
_____
_____
_____
_____
_____
_____
_____
_____

Body Talk

Learning to read and understand someone's body language could be as useful as learning to read and understand their facial expressions. The face, after all, is just another part of the body. So why single out one facet when body language can convey just as much? Ex-FBI agent Joe Navarro is an expert in this field and has taught others about the wealth of information people share without speaking.

Like facial expressions, these tells may indicate deceit or lies, but they mostly indicate discomfort or a discrepancy between feelings and words. With an understanding of body language, we can open new channels of communication and pay attention to our own bodies and the messages we may be unwittingly sending.

In the book, it is explained that the body language theory's central idea is that limbs and gestures may indicate unconscious attempts to protect and defend the body. The limbic brain has reflexes that protect the torso, which has all the body's vital organs, from threats, even emotional ones.

If someone feels attacked, they may cross their arms and say, "Back off." In an argument, raising the arms to the chest is a classic blocking gesture, almost as if the words being exchanged were being thrown. Similarly, slumping arms can indicate defeat, disappointment, or despair.

Think of someone leaning back from a desk with their arms outstretched. Does it make you think of a territorial animal? Broad gestures communicate assurance, dominance, and assertiveness. If you stand with your arms at your sides, your midsection will be on display. This demonstrates that they are not afraid of being in the spotlight.

Meanwhile, the "hand steepling" gesture is widely used by politicians and businesspeople to project authority and confidence. By squeezing the index and middle fingers together, one can make a steeple. It's the universal sign for asserting one's authority and power in a negotiation.

Aside from our hands, our feet and legs can also give some information. The constant motion of one's feet may be an indication of an underlying need to get up and go. It's also been said that people's feet unconsciously point in the direction of their dreams. Turning both feet to face the other person in a conversation can convey "I'm listening to you," while pointing toes outward can indicate a desire to leave.

Are you ready to be a body language master? Answer the questions below:

Evaluate how you read body language. Which specific parts of the body do you tend to look at? When you interact with others, how often do you observe how their body moves? Do you think these movements reveal more about them than their facial expressions?

_____

_____

_____

_____

_____

_____

_____

_____

_____

_____

_____

_____

_____

_____

_____

_____

_____

_____

_____

_____

If someone feels stressed or threatened, what kind of movements does their body make? Do you see the same movement in yourself when you feel the same way?

_____
_____
_____
_____
_____
_____
_____
_____

Imagine walking downtown and seeing two people in front of a bookstore. If one has open hands, while the other has their hands on their chest, what would be your interpretation of their body language? What kind of relationship are they sharing?

_____
_____
_____
_____
_____
_____
_____
_____

Suppose you are in charge of the team meeting. If three of your coworkers are twirling their hair and one of them is pulling the collar of their shirt away from their neck, what do you think their body language is telling you?

_____
_____
_____
_____
_____
_____
_____

How would you picture the body language of a confident politician? Draw it below:

Imagine asking a friend about their condition and they tell you they're fine. If they're telling the truth, what will be their body language? How about when they're lying?

_____
_____
_____
_____
_____
_____
_____
_____

How can you become more conscious of someone's body language in daily interactions? Which body movements will you be more focused on looking at now?

_____
_____
_____
_____
_____
_____
_____
_____

Putting It All Together

All humans constantly engage in nonverbal exchanges with one another. It's not only possible to watch this data unfold in real time, but also to acquire the skills necessary to properly synthesize and interpret it. Do not worry if you are not perfect or an expert at what you are doing. All it takes is a little bit of extra attention and interest in the lives of your fellow humans.

As what is mentioned in the book, you can improve your ability to read people's body language by keeping in mind the following guidelines:

Establish normal behavior.

One or two gestures is not enough to conclude someone's behavior, because they might be accidental or just physiological. But the more you know about someone's "typical" behavior, the more likely you are to believe that any deviation from this norm warrants further investigation.

Imagine meeting your boss for the first time. If your boss is straight-faced and their body language is a bit closed (crossed arms, crossed legs, and monotone voice), what is your first impression of them? Do you think those one or two gestures are enough information to support your impression?

_____
_____
_____
_____
_____
_____
_____
_____
_____
_____
_____
_____
_____
_____
_____
_____
_____
_____

Imagine giving someone a gift and you see them suddenly frown upon opening it. The first thought that comes into your mind is that they hate your gift. Is one facial expression enough to conclude this? How would you verify your conclusion?

_____
_____
_____
_____
_____
_____
_____
_____

How can you ensure not to misjudge someone based on one or two gestures from them? What will you do to get an idea about someone's normal behavior?

_____
_____
_____
_____
_____
_____
_____
_____

Look for unusual or incongruent behavior.

Look closely at the actions that don't fit the context. What you can learn about a person goes beyond what can be gleaned from observing their nonverbal cues alone, thanks to the information contained in the gaps between the two forms of communication.

If someone says "yes" to a party invite but looks down and trembles a lot, what do you think they are trying to really say?

_____

_____

_____

_____

_____

_____

_____

_____

_____

_____

_____

_____

_____

How will you spot an unusual or incongruent behavior the next time you read someone? What signs will you take into account? What will you ignore?

_____

_____

_____

_____

_____

_____

_____

_____

Gather plenty of data.

Remember what you see, but don't jump to conclusions. Verify if they repeat the action. Examine the surrounding context for additional gestures that could corroborate your observations or provide evidence supporting an alternative reading.

Imagine meeting your colleague for the first time. When you had lunch with them, you noticed that they lashed out at the waiter who spilled coffee on them. That same day, during dinner, a waiter spilled water on them. You were expecting them to lash out just like they did during lunch,

but to your surprise, they didn't even get angry at the waiter. Based on this data, what is your "reading" about your colleague?

_____
_____
_____
_____
_____
_____
_____
_____

How do you intend to get more information about someone? Besides body language and facial expressions, what kind of data will you need to form an accurate reading of them?

_____
_____
_____
_____
_____
_____
_____
_____
_____
_____

Look for mirroring.

Remember that gestures may mean one thing in one context or to one person but something else in another context or to someone else. We tend to match and mimic the behavior and expressions of those we like or agree with, but not those we dislike or perceive negatively.

If someone reflects your body posture while you're speaking with them, what do you think they are telling you? Do they like you or not? Why do you think so?

_____

_____

_____

_____

_____

_____

_____

_____

_____

_____

_____

_____

_____

_____

How can you be more conscious when someone is mirroring you? What would you observe first when talking to someone?

_____

_____

_____

_____

_____

_____

_____

_____

_____

_____

_____

Pay attention to energy.

Reading energy means knowing that the loudest voice in a room isn't always the strongest. By looking at where energy flows in a group, you can learn a lot about how power is distributed. Who's the loudest? Who is everyone always talking to, and how? Who always seems to be in the "center of the action"?

Imagine having a group session with your teammates. If someone always wants to be in the corner of the room and only speaks up when spoken to directly, what kind of vibe do they give off? Do you sense a high or low energy from them?

_____

_____

_____

_____

_____

_____

_____

_____

Think of your social circle. Which friend do you think has the highest energy? How about the lowest energy? How did you come up with that judgment?

_____

_____

_____

_____

_____

_____

_____

_____

When in a group, how can you better gauge the energy of each member? What will be your primary points of focus?

_____

_____

_____

_____

_____

_____

_____

_____

_____

_____

_____

_____

_____

Remember that body language is dynamic.

Like verbal information, nonverbal information can vary in delivery. Gestures are living expressions that change over time. Track information in real-time. Look at how expressions change in response to the environment and people. Watch the flow of gestures rather than trying to "catch" one.

If someone confidently talks in long sentences but has a slow, shuffling gait, what kind of person do you think they are? Why?

_____

_____

_____

_____

_____

_____

_____

_____

How can you improve your ability to focus on what others are saying to you as well as the body language they're using?

_____

_____

_____

_____

_____

_____

_____

_____

_____

_____

_____

_____

Context is everything.

Finally, gestures never happen alone. Verbal and nonverbal communication must be considered together. Learn a person's behavior patterns over time, in different contexts, and toward different people.

Now that you've been refreshed with the guidelines, let's reflect on how it can help you become a better people-reader:

If someone is really an "introvert", what do you think their pattern of behavior? What verbal and nonverbal factors should you consider before concluding that someone is an "introvert"?

_____

_____

_____

_____

_____

_____

_____

_____

_____

_____

_____

Imagine observing a friend who has shown inappropriate behavior when you are playing online games with them. He tends to swear a lot and speaks foul of others. You are close to reading him as an aggressive person, but your data is not enough. Aside from his online game behavior, what signs should you also look into to support your assumption?

_____

_____

_____

_____

_____

_____

_____

_____

_____

_____

_____

_____

_____

_____

_____

_____

_____

_____

_____

After reading the guidelines, how will you apply them to become a better people-reader? Which of these guidelines have you been doing already? Which of them do you still need to improve?

_____

_____

_____

_____

_____

_____

_____

_____

The Human Body Is a Whole—Read It that Way

In the previous sections, we've talked about how a person can be "read" on factors that we see, such as their facial expressions and body movements. This time, let's talk about what we hear.

Wim Pouw thinks that people can unconsciously pick up on small but important changes in pitch, volume, and speed of the voice that come with different gestures. Your whole body, including your voice, is involved when you make a gesture. In other words, when you hear someone's voice, you hear different parts of their body.

When you speak, sound travels through all of your body's connective tissues. However, when we make gestures with other parts of our bodies, the muscle tension changes, and we can hear these small changes in the voice. The great thing about this skill is that you don't have to practice it, you just have to know about it. You probably never thought you could practice reading body language over the phone, but you can if you realize that a person's voice is just another part of their body.

Voice is a very rich way to study behavior on its own. Close your eyes when you hear someone in another room, on a recording, or over the phone, and try to picture what their body is doing and what that might mean. You can definitely tell a person's age and gender by listening to their voice, but you can also figure out something about their race or country of origin by listening to their accent or vocabulary.

Pay attention to the speed, tone, volume, pitch, and amount of control. What is the person doing to breathe? How do their words and the way they say them support or hurt each other?

Earlier, we practiced reading people based on what we see. Now, let's boost your listening skills:

When you listen to people, how much do you observe their voice? Do you think that someone's voice can reveal something else about the person? Why or why not?

_____
_____
_____
_____
_____
_____
_____
_____
_____
_____
_____
_____
_____

Imagine you are a customer service representative for a flower company. If someone calls to order flowers for a sick friend, what would they sound like? Would they speak fast or slow? Would they use complicated or simple words?

_____

_____

_____

_____

_____

_____

_____

How would you picture this person you are talking to? What is their body language and facial expression? With this knowledge, would you make some changes to the way you communicate with them?

_____

_____

_____

_____

_____

_____

_____

_____

How can you tell if you are speaking to a scammer over the phone? What would their voice sound like? How fast would they speak? Would they speak in a high or low pitch?

_____
_____
_____
_____
_____
_____
_____

Imagine a happy person who just received a promotion that they've been waiting for, for almost five years. If you talked to them on the phone, what would their voice sound like? How would they breathe? What kind of words would they say?

_____
_____
_____
_____
_____
_____
_____

Is voice alone accurate in interpreting someone's personality? What other factors can you consider if you are reading someone based on their verbal communication?

_____

_____

_____

_____

_____

_____

_____

_____

Have you found that listening to a person's voice, rather than just their words, enables you to better understand and anticipate their actions? Why or why not?

_____

_____

_____

_____

_____

_____

_____

_____

How do you plan to be keener on observing someone's verbal cues? When hearing someone speak, what would you take note of so that you can read their behavior?

_____

_____

_____

_____

_____

_____

_____

_____

Thinking in Terms of Message Clusters

For the previous topics, we have focused on isolated actions. This time let's move to the human behavior's overall message. Do you agree that if we're feeling confident, our language, actions, facial expressions, and voice will reflect this?

Let's examine some traits and the group of behaviors behind them:

Confronting gestures, or those that move actively and energetically toward a target, show **aggression**. Invasive, approaching gestures can indicate an attempt to control, dominate, or attack. This could be a verbal insult or a physical display of superior strength. Aggression is sudden, impactful, and targeted. It's as if the body is clenched around a single goal.

Assertive body language is forceful but not directed. Standing their ground means being firm, balanced, smooth, and open in expressing a confident desire. An assertive person may speak calmly, while an aggressive one may yell.

Submissive body language is usually shown through "lowering" gestures that make the person seem smaller, like smiling a lot, standing still, speaking quietly, looking down, or taking a vulnerable or non-threatening stance.

Open and receptive body language is displayed by keeping their arms and legs open and not crossing them, making natural facial expressions, speaking easily, or even taking off or loosening outer layers of clothing.

Romantic body language focuses on sensuality and connection, such as touching the other person or oneself, preening, stroking, slowing down, and giving warm smiles (prolonged eye contact, questions, agreement, mirroring). Most people think it looks like an invitation to get closer.

Lastly, **deceptive** body language always shows tension. When someone says one thing but believes another, for example, they are being dishonest. Look for the tension that a difference like this makes. You should look for signs of anxiety, closed body language, and distraction.

Based on the examples above, we can read the body by examining communication intentions. This makes it easier to quickly gather multiple data points and find behavioral patterns rather than inferring too much from a single gesture or expression. Consider the entire human body—limbs, face, voice, posture, torso, clothing, hair, hands, fingers, everything:

When you read people, do you take a look at them as a whole? Or do you tend to judge based on gestures or expressions only? Is it better to put cues together or rely on one sign?

_____
_____
_____
_____
_____
_____
_____
_____

Think of a person that you consider kind and compassionate. How did you come up with that conclusion? What did you show for you to think of them that way? What are the patterns of their behavior that you have observed?

_____
_____
_____
_____
_____
_____
_____
_____

If someone is an assertive person, what would be their overall behavior? What kind of gestures do they show? How do they speak? How does their body move?

_____

_____

_____

_____

_____

_____

_____

_____

_____

_____

_____

_____

_____

_____

_____

_____

_____

_____

_____

_____

_____

_____

_____

Imagine being on a first date. Your date is very active in leading the conversation. They are friendly and easy to talk to. As they talk, you notice that they like talking with their hands. Their face is pretty relaxed too.

If your date is doing all of these behaviors, what message are they sending to you?

_____

_____

_____

_____

_____

_____

_____

_____

_____

_____

_____

_____

_____

_____

_____

_____

_____

_____

Think of a few deceptive people, real or fictional. What do you think they have in common in terms of body language? In gestures? In facial expressions? In behavior?

_____
_____
_____
_____
_____
_____
_____
_____

After learning about the clusters of behavior, how will you evaluate people's behavior now? What will you change in your ways to uncover someone's pattern?

_____
_____
_____
_____
_____
_____
_____
_____
_____

Takeaways

- When we read people through observation, we mainly focus on two main areas: facial expressions and body language. It's important to note that even though many things have been scientifically proven (with physiological roots), we can't say that simple observations are foolproof. It can never be definite because there are too many outside factors to take into account. But we can learn what typical things to look for and what we can learn from them.
- Our faces can convey both subtle and obvious emotions. A macroexpression is a much larger, slower, and more pronounced expression. The majority of them are also fabricated and manufactured on purpose. As opposed to these, microexpressions are instantaneous, nearly imperceptible, and subconscious. Psychologist Paul Ekman has identified a wide variety of microexpressions for each of the six basic emotions, as well as

microexpressions that reveal dishonesty or nervousness.

- In contrast, the range of meanings conveyed by body language is much greater. Relaxed bodies tend to take up more room, while anxious ones shrink in on themselves in an effort to feel safe and secure. The only reliable method of analyzing body language is to first know exactly what someone is like when they are normal, but there are too many details to list in a bullet point.

- To make sense of the whole, we need to take a holistic view of the body and search for broad patterns of behavior that serve to convey a consistent message. One's vocal tone can be interpreted similarly to how one might interpret other forms of body language. Look for signs or cues that don't fit in with the other cues they're giving; if you can notice other cues that confirm this conclusion, this may reveal that the other person is trying to hide something. It's possible that the clues you've noticed are meaningless, so you should always double-check your assumptions.

Chapter 3. Personality Science and Typology

Personality can be thought of in the same way as any other facet of a person's communication, behavior, or speech: as an unfiltered window into their complete being. The term "personality" refers to a person's long-term pattern of behavior. A gesture or tone of voice may reveal something about the person, but when it is consistently and frequently displayed, it begins to form the person's identity.

Knowing even a sliver of the general, long-lasting pattern of behavior can provide invaluable context for making sense of the particular behavior we observe at any given time. In psychology, a person's personality is typically seen as a unique combination of their individual features.

Most theories of personality seek to understand the primary ways in which people differ from one another. By doing so, one hopes to get a deeper understanding of human behavior and, ultimately, the ability to predict the likely outcomes of situations.

In the following sections, you will be able to read people through their personalities. But before we jump into that, let's reflect on how you view personality:

What do you think about personality in general? Is it fixed or always changing? Why or why not?

_____
_____
_____
_____
_____
_____
_____

Think of a fictional character and describe their personality. How did you come up with that description? Does their personality predict their actions?

_____
_____
_____
_____
_____
_____
_____
_____

If you know someone's personality, what will change in how you interact with them? Would it be easier or harder for you to approach them? Why or why not?

_____

_____

_____

_____

_____

_____

_____

_____

_____

What are you looking forward to learning about personality that you can apply in reading nonverbal clues?

_____

_____

_____

_____

_____

_____

_____

_____

_____

Test Your Personality

When "personality" is the topic, you might have heard these famous assessments: The Big Five, the Meyers-Briggs Type Indicator, and the Keirsey Temperaments. However, if these tests can be relied upon to give correct results, then there are no more indirect techniques to discover someone's identity.

Very rarely will you have this much information about someone you want to read about or analyze, but again, it's good to know a few different ways to know someone's personality. You might be able to see some of these traits in other people and then figure out what drives them and what they value.

When you were curious about your own personality, you probably took a personality test at some point in your life to learn more about yourself. In terms of analyzing people, this won't get us quite where we want to go. Using these personality tests almost defeats the point of analyzing someone based on what you see and how they act, but they do give you a lot to think about in terms of what traits to look for and what makes people different.

For instance, maybe you experienced being analyzed based on your Big Five personality traits. As mentioned in the book, this is one personality theory that divides the human mind into five main parts. In the same way that emotions can be broken down into "primary colors," and then more complex emotions can be understood as blends of these "primary colors," we can find the five most basic human traits and mix them to explain the rich, colorful differences between people.

Have you taken any of the tests mentioned above? If yes, what result did you get? Do you agree with it? Why or why not?

_____

_____

_____

_____

_____

_____

_____

Are personality tests or assessments reliable in general? What can you say are its advantages and disadvantages?

_____

_____

_____

_____

_____

_____

_____

_____

_____

Among the personality tests mentioned above, which of them do you think provides the most information about someone's personality?

_____

_____

_____

_____

_____

_____

_____

_____

_____

_____

The Big Five

This idea first appeared in D.W. Fiske's published research in 1949. Since then, authors like Norman (1967), Smith (1967), Goldberg (1981), and McCrae and Costa (1987) have discussed its growing popularity. This idea simplifies you down to five characteristics rather than evaluating you as a person based on your experiences and motives. These characteristics include your openness to experience, conscientiousness, extroversion, agreeableness, and neuroticism.

Factor analyses (a statistical method for identifying the fewest factors responsible for the observed variation in data) consistently reveal these same five characteristics to be significant predictors of success (Goldberg, 1993). Although Girven et al. (2012) found the theory to be more applicable to urban and literate cultures, they found that it was less applicable to certain indigenous communities.

Some of these characteristics may be familiar to you. These days, you hear terms like "introvert" and "extrovert." They represent polar opposites on the scale. Each characteristic has a pair of polar opposites, and no matter how much we deny it, we all exhibit some combination of the five characteristics listed below. This hypothesis suggests that our individuality is determined by how much of each trait we exhibit and where we fall within the range between the extremes.

Openness to Experience. One's risk-taking and openness to new experiences are both influenced by Big Five characteristics. If the person you're interested in is likely to participate in an extreme sport or to travel around the world to learn about new cultures, they have a high level of openness to new experiences. They like to look into the dark corners of life.

Conscientiousness. This aspect of personality is what makes someone wary and cautious. If something isn't in their initial plans, they give it some serious consideration before acting on it.

Extroversion. One's level of extroversion is the characteristic that best describes their sociable nature. It's not hard to detect an extrovert. You can always count on them to liven up the room with their boundless enthusiasm and wit. Those who are extroverts get their juice from interacting with others and revel in the spotlight. That's why they keep a large group of friends and seize any chance they get to expand it.

Agreeableness. This reveals how empathetic, friendly, and willing someone is to work with others. Do they tend to worry excessively about the welfare of others? When they see other people going through hard times, how do they react?

Neuroticism. There are days when it feels like nothing is as it seems, and we've all been there. We may feel as though everyone in the office is plotting against us. We may have reached the point of total insomnia due to our excessive worry. But if someone experiences many such days to the extent that they feel sad more often than happy, they may have high levels of neuroticism, the fifth and final Big Five trait. This characteristic is a proxy for one's level of emotional steadiness. It reveals whether or not you tend to be worried, insecure, or easily distracted, and how well someone can maintain a level head in stressful situations.

Finally, we have five characteristics that have been shown to be at least somewhat reliable indicators of important aspects of people's personalities. But how can you use this in people-reading?

Imagine you are mentoring a new colleague. At first, you can observe how easily worried they are whenever there is a new task. You thought that it was just a result of adjusting to a new workplace, so you just shoved it off.

However, a month has passed, and you notice that the trait is consistent. When given a work task, they find it difficult to calm down. They also start to complain constantly, and every day is just a stressful day for them. Sure, they hit the deadlines, but they just emit this dark vibe whenever they're in the office.

Based on the Big Five characteristics, you understand that the person has a high level of neuroticism. They have some difficulty keeping themselves emotionally steady. Using this knowledge, instead of viewing them as someone who just gives off bad energy, you understand that it's their personality. To ease their worry, you give them simple reassurances rather than criticize them for ranting.

Now that you have a better understanding of these characteristics, it is time to put them to use in your ability to read other people:

Think of a person you really want to understand. If they took the Big Five test, which of the traits do you think they scored highest on? How about the lowest?

_____

_____

_____

_____

_____

_____

_____

If someone seems to have a high level of conscientiousness, what is their behavior like? Will they be easy to get along with for you?

_____

_____

_____

_____

_____

_____

Imagine that you are managing an employee who has a low level of agreeableness. Because they are used to doing things alone, you notice that they don't work well in a team. However, you have an upcoming project that requires teamwork. How would you convince your employee to cooperate with their teammates?

_____

_____

_____

_____

_____

_____

_____

If someone has a low score in openness to experience, what will they be like when they are invited to a social event?

_____

_____

_____

_____

_____

_____

_____

_____

_____

_____

If someone is highly neurotic, what will their behavior be when they experience extreme stress?

_____

_____

_____

_____

_____

_____

_____

_____

_____

_____

After learning the Big Five, how can you apply it in reading people's personalities?

_____
_____
_____
_____
_____
_____
_____
_____
_____

Jung and the MBTI

INFP, ESTJ, ISTP, ENTP: You may have seen these random letters on someone's bio while you were viewing their Instagram or Tiktok profile. Or maybe a friend who loves personality tests suddenly asks you, "What is your MBTI type?"

The MBTI is a popular personality test, and people have compared it to the modern horoscope. Similar to the Big Five traits, the test is based on four dichotomies. Of course, no test is perfect, but it can still reveal a person's character or identity.

The MBTI was created during World War II. Myers and Briggs were housewives who saw many people randomly taking jobs. It bothered them that many of those people were working jobs unrelated to their skills. Carl Jung, a psychologist, believed that archetypes were models of people's behaviors and personalities. He strongly implied that these archetypes are innate in human behavior.

Thus, the MBTI was created to help people find careers that matched their personalities. Four general dichotomies or traits are:

• For personality, the spectrum is extroverted (E) to introverted (I).

• For perception, the spectrum is sensing (S) to intuition (N).

• For judging, the spectrum is thinking (T) to feeling (F).

• For implementation, the spectrum is judging (J) to perceiving (P).

All you have to do is take a self-assessment across these four dimensions, and based on the results, you can deduce your personality type.

The first dichotomy, extroversion (E) versus introversion (I), indicates energy source and direction. Extroverts express energy externally. Extroverts recharge in groups. Introverts get energy from within. Recharging that energy is best done in solitude.

Introverts contemplate, while extroverts take action. Students who tend to be more outgoing thrive in classroom settings that encourage group work and public speaking. Student interactions spark changes in their identities. Introverted students often struggle to participate in group projects and feel more at ease working alone. They take pride in their capacity for impartial evaluation.

The second dichotomy describes the different ways that people take in data:

sensing (S) versus intuition (I). When a person is in a sensing state, they are more likely to put stock in data that has been collected through direct experience with the external environment. One way a person can do this is by making use of all five of his or her senses: sight, smell, touch, taste, and hearing. There is a shift toward making decisions quickly and based on past experience. A person who relies on their intuition does not give equal weight to evidence gathered from the outside world. Having a "gut feeling" is one example of this. The individual investigates the situation in greater depth and looks for recurring themes. Until more information is gathered, a conclusion may be delayed.

Sensing involves trusting information that is more concrete and tangible than intuition, which involves looking at the underlying theories or principles that may come out of data. Given the quantifiable nature of evidence and data, a police officer will always use them to back up their claims when making an arrest. In contrast, a lawyer's intuitive nature is useful for defending his clients because there may be more to the story than meets the eye.

A person's mode of information processing is at the center of the third dichotomy: thinking (T) versus feeling (F). Thinking is the process by which a person primarily uses reason to arrive at a choice. They are also ruled by rules and place a focus on the material world when making decisions.

On the other hand, there's the view that prefers relying on gut instinct when making important life choices. These individuals use their core values to guide them toward the most suitable option when faced with a choice. They might label intellectuals as icy and heartless.

For example, homebuyers can be roughly put into two groups: those who buy based on price and resale value (those who think), and those who buy to stay in their current neighborhoods (those who feel).

The fourth dichotomy is judging (J) versus perceiving (P), which refers to how someone will use the data he or she has gathered.

Someone would evaluate it and then use it as a guideline to organize their life so that they could follow it. These folks appreciate rules and routines. They have a high degree of autonomy because they can exert dominion over their environments. People who are inclined to make snap decisions based on their past experiences are called "judging types." They favor final resolutions because of this same sentiment.

On the other hand, if someone loves improvisation and the examination of alternative courses of action, they are of the "perceiving" type. These individuals value freedom of choice and view hierarchy as stifling creativity. They take pleasure in pondering options and developing strategies when faced with a decision.

So, how can you find out someone's MBTI without asking them? Per dichotomy, pick one letter that represents it. To make this easier for you, let's find out the MBTI type of the person mentioned below:

When you attended a social gathering, you approached a girl in a corner named Sarah. At first, you thought that she wasn't enjoying it, but when you struck up a conversation with her, you were able to discover some information.

When you asked Sarah about how she recharges on a tiring day, she said that she loves to recharge alone and enjoys solitary activities. Hearing this, you automatically think of them as an introvert (I).

Then, when you mention some details about yourself, you notice that she processes everything internally before first asking you some follow-up questions to learn more about you. This makes her an intuitive (N) person.

Next, you both are talking about your recent purchases when she reveals that she bought a condominium because she thinks it's a good investment. Because she didn't decide based on feelings, she is a "thinking" (T) type.

Lastly, when you ask her when you can see her again, she takes out her phone and scrolls through her calendar, which is filled with tabs. She mentions that she has a lot of commitments for that month, but says the following month is free. Seeing her organized calendar, you know she is definitely a "judging" (J) type.

Combining all the letters, we get INTJ. Sarah is an introverted, intuitive, thinking, and judging type. According to 16personalities.com, INTJs are called the "Architect" types. They are strategic thinkers who are always looking for ways to improve, and they do so by bringing their unique blend of imagination and logic to bear on every challenge they face. The people they truly are reside in a private, intricate inner world.

So how does this apply to reading people? To illustrate, imagine that your friend declined your spontaneous invitation. Given your familiarity with the INTJ personality type, you don't take the rejection personally and respect that they would likely accept invitations more if they were made a week ahead.

This time, let's try using the MBTI in assessing someone's personality:

If you want to know whether someone is an introvert or extrovert, what will you observe in their words or actions? What question will you ask?

_____

_____

_____

_____

_____

_____

_____

Imagine asking someone to describe their childhood and they respond with this: "When I was a child, I strongly remember the scent of my mom's perfume. I also recall that she loved wearing a pink coat when she brought me to school." Is the person an intuitive (N) or sensing (S) type? Explain.

_____

_____

_____

_____

_____

_____

_____

When making a big life decision, who do you think you would run to for sound advice? A Thinking (T) type or a Feeling (F) type? Why?

_____

_____

_____

_____

_____

_____

_____

_____

_____

_____

_____

_____

_____

_____

_____

_____

_____

_____

_____

_____

_____

Imagine that you have a sister who keeps making promises and then forgetting them quickly afterward. One time, she schedules a dinner with you but failed to make it to the restaurant because, as usual, she forgot your plan to meet. Because of these patterns, you realize that your sister is a perceiving (P) type.

How would you approach her the next time she forgets an appointment with you?

_____

_____

_____

_____

_____

_____

_____

_____

_____

_____

_____

_____

_____

_____

_____

If someone enjoys socializing as a means of recharging their batteries, looks at the big picture, bases decisions on reason, and can't get enough of making plans for the future, what do you think is their MBTI type?

_____
_____
_____
_____
_____
_____
_____
_____

Out of the sixteen personality types, which do you think are the most easiest to deal with? Which are the most challenging to deal with? Explain.

_____
_____
_____
_____
_____
_____
_____
_____
_____

How can you apply the concepts in MBTI in reading people's personality? Without relying on the test, how will you determine whether someone is an introvert or extrovert, sensing or intuiting, feeling or thinking, and judging or perceiving?

_____

_____

_____

_____

_____

_____

_____

_____

Keirsey's Temperaments

The four temperaments described by David Keirsey are often used as a framework for interpreting MBTI results. After assisting in the organization of the MBTI's information, he was able to reduce the sixteen personality types to four overarching temperaments. _Please Understand Me_, published in 1978, is credited with popularizing the concept of temperaments. After WWII, Keirsey became interested in the subject, and he read Ernst Kretschmer and William Sheldon before being introduced to the MBTI in 1956. There is some agreement between the temperaments and the MBTI types, despite a few key differences.

The concept of four basic temperaments has been with us at least since the time of the ancient Greeks, though some have argued that the MBTI and Keirsey's temperaments are pseudoscience (Lilienfeld et al., 2014). Positive correlations were found between the Keirsey Temperament Sorter and the Myers-Briggs Type Indicator in a 2001 peer-reviewed study published in the *Journal of Career Assessment*, suggesting that Keirsey's framework was just as valid as the MBTI.

Figuring out someone's temperament based on their MBTI type is simple: Just consider the two letters in the middle. For instance, if someone is an INFP, you could say their temperament is NF, meaning they scored highly in intuition and feeling. This combination makes them an idealist, someone who values individuality.

Here is the complete list of temperaments:

Temperament One: The Guardian

When someone is both a sensor (S) and judger (J), this is the result. People like this want to make a difference in the world, have faith in themselves, and know they can succeed.

Protectors are also more structured and grounded in reality. People want to feel safe and like they belong, but they also care about doing their jobs. One of their many strengths is their proficiency in logistics, including planning, coordinating, facilitating, supporting, and checking. They can be classed as either administrators or conservators.

The difference between an administrator and a conservator is that the former takes the lead and is more directive. As administrators, they excel. On the other hand, conservators are reactive and expressive.

Temperament Two: The Artisan

When a person scores high on sensing (S) and perceiving (P), this is the result. These people have a very open lifestyle and experience a lot of exciting events.

Artisans have unlimited flexibility. Stimulation and virtuosity are typically what they look for. Making a big splash is important to artisans, and their tactical prowess is one of their greatest strengths. They are highly skilled in debugging, problem-solving, and adaptability. They are also skilled in the use of various implements. They have two roles—operators and entertainers.

Operators are the commanding and proactive artisans. Their speed is unparalleled, and they are also the role variants' most careful designers and advocates. Entertainers, on the other hand, provide more information and are quicker to respond to audience reactions. They are skilled at coming up with solutions on the spot and paying close attention to the smallest of details.

Temperament Three: The Idealist

If someone is both an intuitive (N) and feeling (F) type, then they are idealists. These individuals discover their life purpose by encouraging others to develop their full potential. They place a premium on standing out from the crowd.

One of an idealist's strengths is their ability to be both idealistic and empathetic. They exert effort in an attempt to find meaning in virtually every experience they have. They worry about developing as people and coming into their own. They can be either mentors or advocates.

Mentors are like idealists but more proactive and authoritative. They excel at shaping the future, and their attentive varying roles as advisors and educators are in high demand. Those who are skilled at mediating are advocates, who are the responsive and informative idealists.

Temperament Four: The Rational

This is a combination of being an intuitive (N) and thinking (T) type. They are highly competent and constantly motivated to learn more. In general, they feel content with themselves.

Rationals are based on facts and ideas. They work hard to be the best at what they do and have self-control. Most of the time, they care about their own knowledge and skills. Their best skill is strategy, and they can use logic to investigate, engineer, think up ideas, theorize, and coordinate. They are both engineers and coordinators.

Coordinators are like proactive and directive versions of rationals. They are good at planning, and their different roles include masterminds and field marshals. Engineers are like reactive and informative versions of rationals.

Overall, temperaments can help people gain insight into who they are and what they can do to improve their lives. Different from temperaments, which go deeper than personality types, personality types simply describe how someone is. Understanding one's temperament enables evaluation and, hopefully, improvement. They know themselves better, so if change is required, they can make it.

Now that you are familiar with the temperaments, let's put it to work:

Out of the four temperaments (guardian, artisan, idealist, rational), which of them do you think is easiest to spot? How about the most difficult?

_____

_____

_____

_____

_____

_____

_____

_____

_____

Think of someone you had an argument with. Where does that person fall in the four types? Based on his or her type, how would you respond to them differently? Explain.

_____
_____
_____
_____
_____
_____
_____
_____
_____
_____
_____
_____
_____
_____
_____
_____
_____
_____
_____
_____
_____
_____
_____

Consider yourself a school student working with a rational partner. After completing a school assignment, your instructor proposes that you redo everything since they disliked it. You readily accept your teacher's conclusion and plan a fresh approach to prevent having the same outcome. However, you noticed that your rational team member was easily depressed because of the result.

How would you approach them? How would you lift their spirits so they could get going?

_____
_____
_____
_____
_____
_____
_____
_____
_____
_____
_____
_____
_____

Imagine you're an HR head at a prestigious tech company. One of the best supervisors just filed their resignation and a replacement should be hired immediately. Among the four types, which of them do you think will make a good technical supervisor? Why?

_____

_____

_____

_____

_____

_____

_____

When describing someone's personality, how much would you rely on Keirsey's temperaments? Explain what worked and what didn't in your opinion. What makes it unique from other personality types?

_____

_____

_____

_____

_____

_____

_____

How can you apply the concepts in Kearsey's temperaments in reading people's personality? How can you spot a guardian, artisan, rational, and idealist in your daily interactions?

_____

_____

_____

_____

_____

_____

_____

_____

_____

The Enneagram

The Enneagram test was created in the 1960s to help people achieve self-actualization. The word describes the nine ways a personality can be laid out and comes from the Greek words for "nine" and "written" or "drawn." This model, like the MBTI, is disputed. Today's Enneagram teachings are based on Oscar Ichazo's 1950s psycho-spiritual teaching and Claudio Naranjo's 1970s work. George Gurdjieff, a

Russian mystic, philosopher, and spiritual teacher, influenced Naranjo's personality theories.

An Enneagram primer for psychiatry residents was published in 2020 by the *American Journal of Psychiatry Residents' Journal*, but it has been largely ignored. The Enneagram is used in business management and in seminars and conferences on workplace interpersonal dynamics despite its mystical origins and failure to impress psychologists.

Many practitioners focus on self-improvement because it forces them to confront their flaws. Its focus is on how and why, not what. Instead of diving into the details, it's helpful to have a broad overview of the Enneagram's possible outcomes and try to identify yourself.

The results of this test can be broken down into nine distinct types:

Type One—The Reformer. These people are honest and concerned with being right. Judgmental and self-righteous are also traits of theirs (Ex. physicians and priests).

Type Two—The Helper. These people want to be loved. They're generous but prideful and manipulative (Ex. teachers, mothers, etc.).

Type Three—The Achiever. These people love praise. They're workaholics, which can make them narcissistic (Ex. students and actors).

Type Four—The Individualist. These people seek meaning and uniqueness in their lives. They're creative but moody and temperamental (Ex. musicians and painters).

Type Five—The Investigator. These people strive for expertise. They're usually objective but tend to isolate (Ex. researchers and detectives).

Type Six—The Loyalist. They plan carefully and are loyal to loved ones. They question everything, making them suspicious and paranoid (Ex. survivalists and police).

Type Seven—The Enthusiast. They're energetic and adventurous. They're reckless and overindulgent because they make the best of everything (Ex. thrill-seekers and actors).

Type Eight—The Challenger. These people need power. They're assertive, which can seem aggressive (Ex. military personnel and overbearing parents).

Type Nine—The Peacemaker. Lastly, these people are stable and mediate situations. They're normally easygoing and accepting of all things. This naivety can blind them to negative events (Ex. grandparents and hippies).

By making people think about themselves, the test might reveal things about their minds that were previously hidden.

These personality tests are a theoretical introduction to reading and analyzing people: understand test scales, observe people, and see where they fit. In the end, you might learn something useful, but there's also a chance you're wrong about people and are trying to force them into categories they don't fit. You may learn something, but you may also misclassify or misinterpret people.

Remember that these theories are models for using them effectively. Models always oversimplify complex phenomena. A personality theory or idea can help explain or understand humans, but you need to keep collecting data and adjusting your perceptions.

Think about your family members. Based on their personality, try to identify which Enneagram type they are. Following this, let them take the test thru the link above. Did you guess all the types right? If not, what do you think went wrong with your analysis of their personality?

_____
_____
_____
_____
_____
_____
_____

How many of the nine different Enneagram types have you encountered in your life? Which of them do you think is the most interesting? Which do you think is the most misunderstood?

_____
_____
_____
_____
_____
_____
_____

Imagine having a friend who tends to be perfectionistic. You observe that they are quickly frustrated when something doesn't live up to their standards. One day, they are renovating their home, and you caught them shouting at a painter who brought the wrong shade of paint. What do you think is their Enneagram type? And how would you pacify them in that situation?

_____
_____
_____
_____
_____
_____
_____
_____
_____
_____
_____
_____
_____
_____
_____
_____
_____

Imagine working with someone who you observe is clearly not okay. During work, you observe that their fingers are trembling, and at times, they bite their nails. When you ask them if something is wrong, they avoid the question and change the topic to work. What do you think is their Enneagram type? And how can you help them be vocal about their problem?

_____

_____

_____

_____

_____

_____

_____

_____

_____

_____

_____

_____

_____

_____

_____

_____

If someone is a Type 6 (loyalist), what would they be like as a friend? What do you think are the pros and cons of this specific type?

_____

_____

_____

_____

_____

_____

_____

_____

_____

If someone wants to have a job in the creative sector where they can express their ideas freely, what do you think is their Enneagram type?

_____

_____

_____

_____

_____

_____

_____

_____

_____

How has your understanding of the nine different Enneagram personality types affected your perspective on humanity in general?

_____

_____

_____

_____

_____

_____

_____

_____

_____

Takeaways

- The first step in learning to analyze people like a psychologist involves looking at different personality tests to see what information can be gleaned from them. Actually, quite a few, though none of them can be considered absolute labels for groups of people. The main value they bring is the opportunity to examine human behavior from a variety of levels and angles.

- One of the earliest attempts to categorize individuals based on their individual traits, rather than on their collective characteristics, was the Big Five personality traits. Openness to experience (willingness to try new things), conscientiousness, extroversion, agreeableness, and neuroticism can all be remembered by the acronym OCEAN.
- The MBTI is helpful as a guide, but sometimes people use it like a horoscope and read what they want to see about themselves into their type. The MBTI is based on four different traits and how much you are or are not each trait. The traits are generally introverted/extroverted (your general attitude toward other people), intuitive/feeling (how you take in information), thinking/feeling (how you process information), and perceiving/judging (how you implement information). As a result, there are sixteen distinct personality types.
- The MBTI gives the same information, but the Keirsey temperaments are a way to organize it. Here, instead of sixteen personality types, there are

only four, and each has two roles. The four temperaments are guardian, artisan, idealist, and rational. Keirsey thought that up to 80 percent of people fell into the first two personality types.

- The last personality test is the Enneagram. It is made up of nine general personality types: the reformer, the helper, the achiever, the individualist, the investigator, the loyalist, the enthusiast, the challenger, and the peacemaker. Each type is made up of a certain set of traits, which is more like how Keirsey's temperaments work.

Chapter 4. Lie Detection 101 (and Caveats)

So far in this workbook, you have practiced people-reading by digging deeper into their motivations, body language, and personality types. It's with these methods that you gain a deeper insight into people and appreciate them more fully.

Let's be honest, though; this "understanding" is not purely motivated by interest. We all want to be able to tell when other people are trying to trick us, keep something from us, or outright lie to us, and this is a legitimate desire for many of us.

Excellent people-reading and discernment skills make one a prized companion, parent, or co-worker. However, it also shields you from the malicious plots of others. The abilities we've discussed so far can be a potent self-defense strategy, whether you're trying to uncover white lies in your personal life, see through underhanded dating tactics, or get to the bottom of someone who wants to actively misdirect you.

Even though you've probably heard this before, it's important to remember: in people-reading, there are no guarantees. You can make observations, come up with theories, and make educated guesses, but no method can guarantee that it will work 100 percent of the time because everyone has their own habits, personality traits, and life experiences.

In this chapter of the workbook, we are going to explore a new method to add to your toolbox—a different perspective from which to analyze your data. Before we examine the methods used by trained liar-detectors, such as federal agents, spies, interrogators, and law enforcement officers, let's evaluate your current lie-detecting skills:

What are the signs that you watch out for to determine whether or not someone is lying to you? Do you think these signs are accurate?

_____

_____

_____

_____

_____

_____

_____

_____

_____

On a scale of 1 to 10, rate your lie-detecting skills. Do you consider yourself a pro? Or is there something else that you feel that you should work on?

_____

_____

_____

_____

_____

_____

_____

_____

_____

What do you consider to be the benefits, as well as the drawbacks, of acquiring the ability to identify lies? Which area of your life (relationships, career, etc.) will benefit the most from this skill?

_____

_____

_____

_____

_____

_____

_____

_____

What are you looking forward to learning about lie detecting that you can apply in your daily life?

_____

_____

_____

_____

_____

_____

_____

_____

The Problem: Uncertainty

People tend to overestimate their ability to spot a liar, much like they overestimate their ability to drive. In fact, regardless of age, education level, gender, or self-assurance, people are terrible at detecting liars, according to a study published in the *Forensic Examiner* journal in 2006. In the end, not even expertly calibrated lie detectors could help.

Another paper published in 2006 in the journal *Personality and Social Psychology Review* claimed that most people, including psychologists and judges, were no better than chance at detecting deception. Based on these calculations, fifty out of every twenty thousand people can spot a liar with an accuracy of 80 percent or higher. Although no one wants to believe they are particularly gullible, a skilled liar can be very convincing.

In order to improve as a human lie detector, you must begin with caution.

Before getting to this chapter, you learned how to read cues (facial expressions, body language, and word choice). However, they always show some degree of variability. That said, the idea that liars will all behave in the same predictable way is flawed because of the wide range of human personalities. While the methods can reveal a lot about the character of an honest person who isn't trying to hide anything, it's a different world when it comes to deception.

Worse yet, the information that would-be lie detectors use is available to the liars as well. The next time you feel the urge to touch your face, remind yourself that people may view this as a sign of suspicion, and refrain from doing it. If the person you're talking to is used to lying or almost believes the story they're telling you, they might not give you any hints at all.

But don't worry, because the problem has a solution. We can actually improve our lie-detection accuracy! The thing is, when we know what to expect and are able to adjust our expectations accordingly, we are better able to read people's intentions and avoid being tricked.

As mentioned in the book, the accuracy of lie detection methods typically increases when:

- You have a solid baseline of behavior against which to compare current behavior
- The person doing the lying is spontaneous, i.e., they haven't had any time to rehearse their lie or prepare themselves
- The lie comes with real consequences for getting caught—this may up the stakes and make liars more nervous

You must remember: There is no single telltale sign or indicator of dishonesty. People's personalities can shift dramatically under stress, with some becoming more talkative than usual or exhibiting tics they've never shown before, and others becoming more serious and easily distracted. Even if you could reliably identify nervousness, you still wouldn't have proof that the person was lying; they might be on edge because they sense your mistrust.

Instead of asking how to get better at spotting deception, we should flip the question and ask if we can figure out why we fall for it in the first place. From this point, we can't do much about the fact that there are liars in the world, but we can examine our own selves to see if there are any traits, attitudes, or practices that make it easier for us to miss signs of deception.

Sometimes, detecting lies can be clouded by our own judgment and biases. For instance, if someone has a personal belief that all religious people are incapable of lying, they might easily fall for a dishonest salesman who uses biblical quotes to convince them to buy a product that isn't even worth its price.

If they can examine their absolute belief about religious people, perhaps they will be more skeptical of a product's value the next time a Bible-quoting man tries to sell it to them.

To improve your lie-detecting skills, it is also essential to learn to spot your own preconceived notions, assumptions, and unconscious biases. Let's uncover what those are through the questions below:

In general, what are your thoughts on the practice of lying? Do you consider it to be completely inappropriate? Or is there a positive aspect to it that we are missing?

_____

_____

_____

_____

_____

_____

_____

_____

_____

Based on what you learned from the previous chapters, what do you think motivates people to lie? Do you think there is a certain personality type that is prone to lying?

_____

_____

_____

_____

_____

_____

_____

_____

_____

If someone lies to you, what is your initial reaction? Do you get furious? Or do you reflect on why they did it? Why do you think you react that way?

_____

_____

_____

_____

_____

_____

_____

_____

_____

If a loving husband lies to his sensitive wife about her weight, what do you think is the reason behind his lying? Do you think that the wife's personality has anything to do with the husband's lying?

_____

_____

_____

_____

_____

_____

_____

_____

_____

Have you ever formed a hasty opinion of someone when you were feeling stressed or anxious? To what extent do you think your opinion of that person would have changed if you'd been feeling better?

_____

_____

_____

_____

_____

_____

_____

_____

_____

Do you stick with what you know when making assumptions about someone? Or do you conduct additional research by soliciting input from others?

_____

_____

_____

_____

_____

_____

_____

_____

_____

How can you be more accurate in spotting lies? Based on what you learned in this section, what will you practice more? What will you avoid doing?

_____

_____

_____

_____

_____

_____

_____

_____

_____

It's All About the Conversation

According to Pamela Meyer's now-famous 2016 TED Talk, "Hot to Spot a Liar," the average person is lied to anywhere from ten thousand to two thousand times per day. In fact, she claims that within the first ten minutes of meeting, people tell three different lies to each other. She listed signs of deceit, such as a tense upper body, more formal language, and other "hot spots" in conversations, such as false smiles and inconsistencies between words and actions.

Obviously, the way you use your body speaks volumes. Yet, a lie is a form of verbal construction; it is a story told in a way that is dynamic, real-time, and always in the presence of another active listener in conversation. There's more to lie detection than keeping a sharp eye out for a few nervous ticks here and there. Working with the entire conversation is essential.

Meyer claims that lying is an act of "cooperation" and that a lie can only be effective if others actively buy into it. She also argues that, as a society, we tend to sanction lying to some extent, despite the fact that most of us publicly declare that we are against lying.

If this is the case, how can we use it to detect deception? Well, we need to start paying attention to the whole social interaction and the cultural setting in which it occurs, not just the individual liar.

You are not a passive observer of conversation; rather, you are an active participant. By asking questions, taking control of the conversation, and subtly applying pressure, you can coax the other person into volunteering information rather than having to go looking for it yourself. Let's rethink the ability to detect lies not as a series of isolated observations but as a conversational skill.

As a refresher, here are some tips from the book. Keep these in mind; you will apply them later.

- **Start with open-ended questions.** To give the other person time to lay out any potentially conflicting facts or threads you can unravel later to prove a lie, let them speak first and often.
- **If you have your own evidence or information, keep it to yourself for as long as possible.** Keep in mind that the person who is lying is in a tough spot. They have to convince you of a story, but they usually don't know what you know.
- **Ask the person a question out of the blue that has nothing to do with what you're talking about.** Then watch to see if they are having trouble coming up with something on the spot. Most of the time, liars also take longer to answer

questions and pause more often while telling their answers.

- **If you see a mistake or even a lie, don't say anything about it. Wait a little bit and watch.** You might get to see the liar actively making up a story right in front of your eyes. When you finally do confront this person with proof of lying, keep an eye on how they react. People who get caught lying may get angry or shut down, but people who are telling the truth may just act a little confused and keep telling the same story.

- Dr. James Drikell, head of the Florida Maxima Corporation, says that when two people are in on a lie, they don't consult with each other and don't elaborate on the other's story, unlike truth-tellers. **If you suspect two people of lying, watch how they interact—honest people are more comfortable and proactive about sharing the story.**

Think back on a time when you discovered someone's dishonesty just by talking to them. How were you able to confirm that they were lying? What did you observe in the way they engaged with you in a conversation?

_____
_____
_____
_____
_____
_____
_____

Imagine you have a partner whom you believe has been unfaithful to you. If he is guilty of being with someone else, what will be different in their actions? What questions will you ask them to confirm if they are lying or not?

_____
_____
_____
_____
_____
_____
_____

Imagine having a son who goes home with a broken arm. When you ask him what happened, he mentions that he got into an accident. If he says this while appearing so tense and can't look you in the eye, what can this mean? How can you make sure that it was really an accident and not because of a school bully?

_____

_____

_____

_____

_____

_____

_____

_____

_____

_____

_____

_____

_____

_____

_____

_____

_____

_____

_____

_____

Think of a fictional character whom you think is a good liar. Observe how they engage with the other characters. What do you think makes them effective in what they do?

_____

_____

_____

_____

_____

_____

_____

Imagine that you are a writer and that you are in the process of creating a fictional character who is a brilliant detective and able to quickly identify lies just through a conversation. What characteristics do you plan to emphasize when developing your character?

_____

_____

_____

_____

_____

_____

_____

How can you determine whether or not a person is making up a story? What kinds of clues will you be looking for?

_____

_____

_____

_____

_____

_____

_____

_____

How can you improve your analysis of body language and conversation when trying to catch a liar? Based on what you learned about lie detection, which of the tips above will you definitely put into practice?

_____

_____

_____

_____

_____

_____

_____

_____

Use the Element of Surprise

People who lie on the spot are the most dishonest. To increase the likelihood of catching the other person in an unnatural and hastily told lie, it is best to set up your questions and conversations with them to occur on the spur of the moment. You are not attempting to determine whether the story you are told is true or false based solely on body language and other nonverbal cues, as you would when using the conversational techniques discussed above. You want the other person to reveal who they really are and fall for their own lies.

We know that asking unexpected questions can throw a liar off their game because they force them to deviate from their prepared answers. Keep an eye out for any unexpected shifts in their level of assurance, the rate at which they speak, or the level of eye contact they maintain with you. Responding vaguely to a yes/no question is a dead giveaway.

If asked a question, a truth-teller won't hesitate to give a straightforward answer. Meanwhile, a liar will either repeat the question or provide an extremely detailed answer.

If you catch someone off guard, they may become temporarily flustered or even react angrily. Keep an eye out for any abrupt changes in emotion or language. To cover their fear, a person may act irrationally angry.

To get to the truth when you suspect someone is lying, it's best to be nonchalant and ask questions quickly so they don't have time to make up a story. If you can do this, a lot of what you've been observing in terms of behavior or body language may suddenly become more useful, such as keeping an eye out for signs of anxiety or attempts to conceal one's identity.

Try to imagine what it's like to be a liar. Consider the hypothetical situation in which you stole money from someone. How do you plan to explain away your possible theft if they ask you, "Did you take my money?"

_____

_____

_____

_____

_____

_____

_____

_____

Based on the lie you constructed above, how did you come up with it? Were you able to come up with a quick excuse? Or did it take a minute or two? What did you observe being in the shoes of a liar?

_____

_____

_____

_____

_____

_____

_____

_____

If someone has lied to you about eating the food that you left in the fridge for yourself, what would their reaction be if you asked them if they ate it?

_____

_____

_____

_____

_____

_____

_____

_____

Imagine Person B canceling their date with Person A last minute because of a sudden family gathering. The next day, their conversation goes like this:

A: Hey, how was your family gathering?

B: Oh, the family gathering? It was great. I saw my cousins again after a long time.

A: Oh, I want to see them! Were you able to take photos?

B: Well, not everyone loves to take photos and post them on social media.

A: You didn't really go, did you?

B: Do you really think I'm lying just because I don't have a photo? Great.

A: Chill. I was just asking if you went or not.

B: Man, this just goes to show how much you don't trust me. I am so done with you.

Based on the conversation, how can you describe Person B's responses and reaction? Are they lying or not? What makes you think so?

_____

_____

_____

_____

_____

_____

_____

_____

_____

_____

_____

_____

_____

_____

_____

_____

In the conversation above, how did Person A use the element of surprise to check if Person B was lying or not?

_____

_____

_____

_____

_____

_____

_____

_____

_____

How can you apply the element of surprise in your daily conversations? What do you think are its advantages and disadvantages?

_____

_____

_____

_____

_____

_____

_____

_____

_____

_____

How to Increase Cognitive Load

The truth is simple to tell; just say what you can remember. Putting together a convincing lie requires more mental effort. Instead of recalling events, you're creating a narrative from scratch, and this story needs to convince. Stressing out a liar until they make a mistake and spill the beans is a surefire way to get the truth out of them.

The best strategy is to avoid acting as if you're in a formal interrogation situation and play the role of a no-nonsense detective. Rather, keep the conversation casual but moving forward. Pay close attention and put some light pressure on the weaker parts of the story. With enough time, you might figure out the story's flaws or notice a major discrepancy. If you press this inconsistency, you might get more dishonesty or deeper, unbridgeable schisms.

It's an intriguing conversation starter to inquire right away as to the other person's level of honesty. People are prompted to be more honest in the future, or at least you'll find a conflict between wanting to appear truthful and actually being dishonest. A person's nerves could cause them to accidentally admit the truth or, at the very least, make a fool of themselves while trying to lie.

In the book, a technique to catch those lies is to increase the liar's cognitive load. By causing the other person to use more mental energy than they have, you can expose their lie. Here is how you can do it:

- **Say something untrue and observe their reaction.** This will show you their baseline response to lies. Try doing this several times, alternating between true and false, and the liar will have to do a lot of mental gymnastics on the spot.
- **If you suspect they are lying, you can ask them to tell you a story you know to be true and then compare it to how they tell it.** You can use this to get a sense of the person's typical demeanor even if you don't know them very well.
- **Ask unexpected questions that will cause them to temporarily abandon the rehearsed story.** They may have forgotten the details when they return to it. Take an insignificant part of the story

and tell it to them again with an extra piece you added or a minor detail incorrect. See what they do. If they truly believe you made a mistake, they may accept the claim for ease.

- **Detect any stiffness, awkwardness, or unnaturalness in the story the liar presents.** If you're far enough into the conversation and the cracks are beginning to show, you might even begin to directly allude to the consequences of being found lying. This can befuddle and stress a person, draining their cognitive resources and increasing the likelihood that they will make a mistake or say something truly heinous.

- **Finally, pay attention to how emotions are expressed during a conversation.** Joe Navarro, an ex-FBI agent and interrogation expert, emphasizes the importance of clusters of behavior rather than individual observations. There is an emotion behind the cognitive fact of the lie: guilt, nervousness, fear, or even a secret thrill at getting away with things.

As the difficulty of your questions increases, so will the expression of emotion. Don't stop narrowing things down. Asking about feelings is a great way to see how people deal with the mental strain of having to recall a story they made up.

Now, let's try to put it into action with the questions below:

If someone is dishonest, would they exert more mental effort than honest people? Why do you think so?

_____
_____
_____
_____
_____
_____
_____
_____

If you want to know if someone is telling the truth or not, what will you do to increase someone's cognitive load?

_____
_____
_____
_____
_____
_____
_____
_____

Consider a person you know for a fact has lied to you in the past. Recall the emotions that they were experiencing while they were lying to you. What have you observed? Do their words match their emotions?

_____

_____

_____

_____

_____

_____

_____

_____

Imagine that you're an FBI agent interviewing two suspects for a murder case. You ask them the same question, "How did you feel when Person C was murdered?"

Person A looks down and sighs deeply with tears on her cheeks, saying that she felt sad to hear about the news. She claims that she had seen Person C that morning but didn't realize that she would be dying that night.

On the other hand, Person B pauses for a second before answering. With a straight face, he mentions that he was surprised because Person C was just alive that morning. He adds that Person C didn't deserve what happened to her because she was a good person, and the murderer must pay for what he did.

Based on their responses, which of them do you think is telling the truth? Which one is lying? Explain how you came up with your conclusion.

_____

_____

_____

_____

_____

_____

_____

_____

_____

_____

_____

_____

_____

_____

_____

_____

If you are unconvinced with both responses, how will you increase their cognitive load so you can confirm if they are lying or not?

_____
_____
_____
_____
_____
_____
_____
_____
_____
_____

How can you improve your lie-detecting skills by increasing the liar's cognitive load? Which of the steps above will you practice more?

_____
_____
_____
_____
_____
_____
_____
_____
_____

General Tips for Better-than-Average Lie-Detecting

So far, you were able to enhance your lie-detecting skills by recognizing your biases, brushing up on your conversational skills, using the element of surprise, and learning how to increase cognitive load. You also learned that lie-detecting isn't just a body language thing; there are a lot of things you should consider before making an accurate judgment.

Before we evaluate your newly honed ability, allow us to go over some general pointers that are important for you to keep in mind as you move forward in your lie-detecting journey.

- Sit back and let the other person volunteer information, rather than pulling it out of them. Don't let on what you know too early—or at all.
- Stay relaxed and causal. What you are observing is not the person themselves, but the person as they are in a quasi-interrogational situation with *you*. So don't make it seem like an inquisition; otherwise, you may

simply be watching them feel distressed about the situation itself.

- Don't worry about individual signs and clues like touching the nose, looking up to the right, or stuttering. Rather, look at how the person responds in general to *shifts* in the conversation, especially at junctures where you believe they may be having to concoct a story on the fly.

- Listen for stories that seem unusually long or detailed—liars use more words, and they may even talk more quickly.

- Take your time. It may be a while before you uncover a deception. But the longer the other person talks, the more chance they have of slipping up or getting their story tangled.

- Watch primarily for inconsistencies— details of the story that don't add up, emotional expressions that don't fit the story, or abrupt shifts in the way the story is told. Being chatty and then all of a sudden getting quiet and serious when you ask a particular question is certainly telling.

- Always interpret your conversation in light of what you already know, the context, and other details you've observed in your interactions with this person. It's all about looking at patterns and then trying to determine if any disruptions in that pattern point to something interesting.

- Don't be afraid to trust your gut instinct! Your unconscious mind may have picked up some data your conscious mind hasn't become aware of. Don't make decisions on intuition alone, but don't dismiss it too quickly, either.

What insights into lying in general have you gained from completing this section of the workbook? Do you now think differently about lying?

_____

_____

_____

_____

_____

_____

_____

_____

Out of the methods you learned, which do you think is the most useful? Which do you think is the least useful? Why?

_____
_____
_____
_____
_____
_____
_____
_____
_____

Now that you have finished this chapter of the workbook, please rate your lie-detecting skills on a scale of 1 to 10. Compared to your initial assessment, what changed?

_____
_____
_____
_____
_____
_____
_____
_____
_____

How can you further improve your lie detection? Which of the strategies that you have picked up will you most likely apply in the interactions that you have in the future?

_____
_____
_____
_____
_____
_____
_____

Takeaways

- Despite widespread belief to the contrary, the average person is not particularly adept at detecting lies. Because of our own preconceived notions, expectations, and biases, it can be difficult to recognize when we are being deceived.
- Detecting lies effectively is a fluid procedure that must center on the conversation. Ask open-ended questions for people to give information. Keep an eye out for

rambling, all-at-once stories, inconsistencies in the story or emotional affect, delays or avoidance in answering questions, and an inability to answer unexpected questions.

- The best way to catch a liar is to catch them in the act of lying. If possible, avoid giving the liar time to practice their lines, or better yet, plant a lie yourself and observe the liar's reaction to determine whether or not they are telling the truth.

- Increasing the liar's cognitive load may cause them to fumble their story or lose track of specifics, thereby exposing their lie. Continue to probe for information and be suspicious if details don't add up, if emotion doesn't match content, or if the person is purposely stalling.

- Keep an eye out for specific indicators of cognitive overload. One example is that the liar will exhibit fewer emotions while speaking than they or the average person would in a similar circumstance. Instead, their body language will reveal their emotions. This typically manifests as increased blinking, dilated pupils, speech disorders, and slips of the tongue.

Chapter 5. Using the Power of Observation

This chapter of the workbook will build on the previous ones, but with one additional factor: time. Your people-reading skills can get better over time, that's for sure. However, the reality is that there are times when we simply do not have the luxury of extra time. Character judgments must be made on the fly.

As you go along, you'll apply techniques for making snap judgments about people based on the limited information provided by their appearance, demeanor, and speech patterns.

Everyone has seen videos of fake psychics and mediums claiming to contact the dead. The medium releases an ill-defined hint into the general public and observes who responds to it. Then, they home in a bit more. If the person is on the older side, they make a nebulous reference to a child or a spouse, knowing that most people of this age will have spouses or children. They get even closer, depending on how they take this new information.

We're not trying to perfect the result, but rather the ethos of the process. When applied correctly, there are scientifically backed methods for making fairly accurate first impressions of people.

You've probably heard of the saying "first impressions last," but do you agree with this statement? Why or why not?

_____
_____
_____
_____
_____
_____

Think of someone you just met recently. What was your first impression of them? What did you observe in that person that formed your impression of them?

_____
_____
_____
_____
_____
_____
_____
_____

What are you looking forward to learning about the power of first impressions that you will definitely apply in your life?

_____

_____

_____

_____

_____

_____

_____

_____

How to Use "Thin-Slicing"

When studying people and their actions, psychologists use a technique called "thin-slicing," which involves looking for patterns in extremely limited data. The term was used for the first time in a paper by psychologists Nalini Ambady and Robert Rosenthal in the journal _Psychological Bulletin_ in 1992. However, the idea of using philosophy and psychology to predict future behavior with little information has been around for a long time.

Psychological research has shown that people's impressions of others don't improve after the first five minutes of meeting them. This could mean that first impressions last or that information is so easy to get that a person can make a good choice in a short amount of time.

Albrechtsen, Meissner, and Susa's 2019 study, which is cited in the book, found that "intuition" is often more accurate than chance at spotting bias or deception in others. Notably, they outperformed those who gave the situation a more analytical and thoughtful evaluation.

Malcolm Gladwell suggested in his best-selling book *Blink: The Power of Thinking Without Thinking*, that one of the reasons snap judgments are made so quickly is because they are largely unconscious. This can be seen in art experts who are quick to spot fake art forms just by taking a single look at them.

Nalini Ambady also found that how we feel can affect how accurate these snap judgments are. For example, being sad makes people less accurate when judging others, which may be because it makes them think about things more carefully.

In the early chapters of this workbook, you learned how to examine your biases and prejudices, and how knee-jerk reactions can interfere with your people-reading. But a good people-reader knows how to utilize both the unconscious and conscious aspects of people-reading—the intuition paired with sound decision-making.

It's best not to overanalyze the situation right away when interacting with a new person. It's enough to simply become aware of your initial reaction; from there, you can let that reaction gently lead you to a more in-depth, reflective consideration. You should feel free to question your first thoughts, but you shouldn't dismiss your gut reaction just because you can't explain it.

In this chapter of the workbook, you will practice using your hunches to your advantage and learn how to thin-slice.

In reading people, is it possible that our intuition is more reliable than the methods you've learned in the earlier chapters (knowing motivations, reading body language and facial cues, personality typing, and lie detecting)? Why?

_____
_____
_____
_____
_____
_____
_____

Recall an instance in which you had a gut feeling about someone that turned out to be correct. What did you suspect? And how did you discover that you were right?

_____
_____
_____
_____
_____
_____
_____

Think back to a time when you trusted your instincts about someone but they turned out to be completely false. What do you think went wrong? Did your emotions interfere with your judgment?

_____

_____

_____

_____

_____

_____

_____

_____

_____

_____

_____

_____

_____

_____

_____

_____

_____

_____

_____

_____

_____

Imagine you're a new student at a university and it's your first day. After meeting all your professors, you notice that you feel "off" with one of them. You can't seem to explain why, but the bad feeling is strong. Having this knee-jerk reaction, what will you do? Will you trust it? Or will you give room for your professor to prove you wrong? Why?

_____

_____

_____

_____

_____

_____

_____

_____

_____

_____

_____

_____

_____

_____

_____

_____

_____

_____

_____

Thin-slice this: You've just met the new romantic partner of your best friend. You notice that they like to take the lead in conversations and rudely cut you off while you're talking. If your best friend's partner acts this way, what is your immediate hunch about this limited information? Do you think they make a good partner for your best friend?

_____

_____

_____

_____

_____

_____

_____

_____

_____

_____

_____

_____

_____

_____

_____

_____

_____

_____

How can you ensure that your thin-slicing is accurate? How will you condition yourself before concluding something out of limited data?

_____

_____

_____

_____

_____

_____

_____

_____

_____

Making Smart Observations

As you can imagine, the quality of the assessments you make from your thin-slice depends a lot on what's in that slice. It would be unfair to assess someone entirely based on a few seconds of data. It's important to choose your data carefully when making these judgments.

Let your brain make snap judgments in the first few seconds you meet someone. As you continue, you can use more deliberate observational methods. Slow down your processing and focus on what they say and what they share. In this section of the workbook, you'll learn how to examine whether emails and social media can reveal a person's personality, and how to decipher their word choice.

Look at the Words People Use

Have you ever formed a negative impression of someone based on the way they worded a text message? When reading an email signature, have you ever been able to deduce the writer's mood, level of education, gender, or personality traits?

According to research published in *Social Influence* in 2006, the use of profanity and swearing can make a speaker seem more passionate and convincing, but it has no effect on the audience's opinion of the speaker's credibility. A related study published in the *Journal of Research in Personality* found that the way a person uses personal pronouns (I, me, mine) is related to how outgoing they are, while the way they use negative emotion words is related to how neurotic and agreeable they are.

The way someone talks can be a window into their state of mind and body. For instance, nervous people tend to express themselves more strongly through negative language. They won't express disapproval if they're irritated. The more common responses are "sick of" or "hate." Optimists are less likely to use negative descriptors like "hate," "disgusting," and "etc." An underlying problem exists if a person's normal response to even mildly upsetting events is to express extreme emotion through words.

Meanwhile, if a person only ever uses "I" statements, that may be an indication of where their attention truly lies. However, Pennebaker and colleagues found something quite intriguing: Depressed people use the pronoun "I" more frequently than non-depressed people do. To make things even more confusing, research by Professor Richard Wiseman has shown that people who tell the truth use the first-person pronoun "I" when making a claim, while people who lie may not do this.

Again, it's important to remember that when analyzing people's word choice, context matters. Instead of expecting language to tell us something definitive on its own, we need to interpret it within a larger pattern. You can tell the difference between someone who uses "I" to narrate their heroic exploits and shower you with their many opinions and someone whose frequent use of "I" serves primarily to apologize or express uncertainty.

In this section of the workbook, you will practice reading other people through their word choices.

Imagine catching up with a friend whom you haven't seen for a decade. During your conversation, you notice that they love using words that aren't easily understandable to the point that you always have to ask what the word means. If someone likes to use complicated words in their speech, what is your assessment about them? What kind of person are they?

_____

_____

_____

_____

_____

_____

_____

_____

_____

_____

_____

_____

_____

_____

_____

_____

_____

Open your inbox and pick one conversation that you would like to analyze. It could be from a romantic interest, a friend, a family member, or a superior—your call. After reading the conversation, answer the following questions below:

Does the person use a lot of pronouns or mostly talk about others? What do you think their pronoun choice says about their personality? ·

_____

_____

_____

_____

_____

_____

_____

_____

_____

_____

_____

_____

_____

_____

_____

_____

When it comes to their word choice, do you think they are more of the emotional or logical type? Which of their words helped you come up with this impression?

_____

_____

_____

_____

_____

_____

_____

_____

_____

Are their words easy to comprehend, or do they tend to use technical language? Why do you think they use it?

_____

_____

_____

_____

_____

_____

_____

_____

_____

How often do they swear? What kind of swear words do they use?

_____

_____

_____

_____

_____

_____

_____

_____

_____

Observe their vocabulary use. Do they struggle in expressing what they mean? Or is it effortless for them to come up with the right word to say what they really want to say? Based on their level of vocabulary, what type of person are they?

_____

_____

_____

_____

_____

_____

_____

_____

_____

_____

Do you think you feel closer to them when you talk to them, or do you think your conversations make them feel more distant?

_____

_____

_____

_____

_____

_____

_____

_____

_____

Pay attention to how they use "you," "your," and "yourself." How often do they use them to encourage and support one another versus to blame and manipulate others?

_____

_____

_____

_____

_____

_____

_____

_____

_____

Do they mimic your language? Do they tend to repeat the words you say? If yes, how does it make you feel?

_____

_____

_____

_____

_____

_____

_____

_____

After doing the exercises above, how can you apply these smart observations in your daily life? When talking to someone, what will you concentrate on analyzing now?

_____

_____

_____

_____

_____

_____

_____

_____

Read People like Sherlock Holmes Reads a Crime Scene

By now, it should be clear that even with limited data, such as a person's word choice, it is possible to get a sense of who they are. The same is true of reading people; all you have to do is observe their body language and facial expressions. The next challenge is connecting all those behind the little clues that you picked up.

In the book, another way to look at people is through their photographs. Dacher Keltner and LeeAnne Harker of the University of California, Berkeley, examined dozens of smiling women in college yearbooks. In their study, two kinds of smiles were discovered: a "Duchenne," or genuine smile, and a "Pan Am," or forced smile. The whole face lifted, the eyes closed, and lines appeared around the mouth and nose. The posed or forced smile was limited to the mouth and did not affect the eyes or facial muscles. Years later, the researchers discovered that people with "Duchenne" smiles are generally happier than people with "Pan Am" smiles.

Besides smiles, clothes can also tell you something about a person. Our clothes are a way to show who we are and how we want other people to see us. It's a powerful way to show our sexual orientation and gender identity, our culture, our age, our socioeconomic status, our jobs, our unique personalities, and even our religious beliefs.

Dr. Jennifer Baumgartner, a psychologist, thinks there should be a "psychology of clothing" because the way people shop and the clothes they wear say a lot about their motivations, values, and how they see themselves. They tell us where we fit in the world, what our status is, and how we interpret how we look.

Now, let's practice reading people through their appearance based on the guidelines in the book:

In appearance-reading, it's important to consider how a person's attire fits with their environment. If you see a person who is wearing tattered jeans and flip-flops going to a party, what kind of message do you think they are sending with their clothing?

_____

_____

_____

_____

_____

_____

_____

_____

_____

_____

_____

_____

_____

_____

_____

_____

_____

_____

_____

_____

Let's investigate how much time and attention a person typically spends caring for their physical appearance. Think about it like this: You're getting ready for a date and you want to look your best. The problem is that when your date finally shows up, they have wrinkled clothes and unruly hair. It's clear they didn't try as hard as you did. If someone appears this way, what do you infer about their confidence level?

_____

_____

_____

_____

_____

_____

_____

_____

_____

_____

_____

_____

_____

_____

_____

_____

_____

Think about your boss or any superior's appearance. How do they show their status through their clothing? What kind of clothes do they wear? What else do they put on to show wealth or power?

_____
_____
_____
_____
_____
_____
_____

If someone wants to draw attention to themselves, what kind of clothing will they most likely wear?

_____
_____
_____
_____
_____
_____
_____
_____
_____
_____

What a person usually wears is a mirror of what they do for a living. Think of a friend who likes to wear the same style or type of clothes. Is it accurate that their type of clothing represents their occupation?

_____

_____

_____

_____

_____

_____

_____

Think of the typical extroverts and introverts. How are their styles of clothes different? How about their choice of colors? What do you observe about their appearance in general?

_____

_____

_____

_____

_____

_____

_____

_____

How will you act like Sherlock Holmes when it comes to reading people? Which of his traits will you most likely embody so you can have accurate readings?

_____

_____

_____

_____

_____

_____

_____

Home and Possessions—Extensions of the Personality

When you go to someone's home, look at it the same way you would look at how they dress, how they move, or what they say. After all, a home is a lot like an extension of who we are as people.

Is the house open and comfortable or messy? Look for signs of friendliness, such as places for guests to congregate and attention to visitors. If a person's house is empty and too clean, it may tell you something about how neurotic they are. If someone has a lot of expensive decorations and pictures of themselves with famous people in gold frames, you can tell that prestige and money are important to them.

Sam Gosling says in his book *Snoop: What Your Stuff Says About You* that you can even figure out a person's political views from the way they decorate their bedroom. He found that American conservatives were more likely to have traditional items like flags and sports memorabilia in their homes. Liberals tended to live in more colorful places.

Most of the time, if a space is too clean and organized, the person who lives there is likely to be conservative because they tend to be careful. On the other hand, liberal spaces shout openness and creativity because the people who live there don't like routine and order.

According to Gosling, possessions and artifacts can be broken down into roughly three categories:

- Those objects that make **identity claims**—items that show our personality, value, or sense of identity directly. Ornaments, posters, awards, photos, jewelry, and adornment (think a gold cross around the neck or a Celtic knot tattoo). Look at the space and ask, "Who lives here? What kind of person owns this item?"

- Objects that act as **feeling regulators**—the things that help people manage their own emotional state. An inspirational quote, a picture of a loved one, sentimental items. These all tell you what the person values and cherishes most.

- Finally, items that are **behavioral residues**—these are the things left behind in the ordinary course of life. These could be things like piles of old Vodka bottles in the corner, an unfinished book next to the sofa, a half-finished craft project on the dining room table. These give you a neat glimpse into people's habits and behaviors.

Using these concepts, let's try to read a person based on reading their space and the stuff they have:

Look at the bedroom above. What vibe do you get just by looking at it? What are the things you liked and disliked about it?

_____

_____

_____

_____

_____

_____

_____

_____

Observe the items found in the bedroom. Which of them do you identify as extensions of their personality (identity claims)? Which are the things they use to manage their emotional state (feeling regulators)? Which are the things that they left behind (behavioral residues)?

_____

_____

_____

_____

_____

_____

_____

_____

Based on your answers above, let's try to read the owner of this room. What do you think is their identity? What kind of person are they? How do they manage their emotions? What could be their habits?

_____

_____

_____

_____

_____

_____

_____

_____

_____

_____

_____

_____

_____

_____

_____

_____

_____

_____

_____

Now, let's examine this room and the stuff in it. If someone has this kind of room, what kind of person do you think lives in this place?

_____
_____
_____
_____
_____
_____
_____
_____

Which of the items do you think says a lot about how they cope with their emotions? What do you think they value and cherish the most?

_____

_____

_____

_____

_____

_____

_____

_____

What are the behavioral residues in the room? Based on those items, what do you think they do for a living?

_____

_____

_____

_____

_____

_____

_____

_____

_____

_____

_____

After reading the two rooms above, what did you learn about the process of analyzing people through their space and possessions that made so much sense? How will you apply this learning in real life?

_____
_____
_____
_____
_____
_____
_____
_____

How to Read People's Behavior Online

You can get a sense of a person's online character from their emails before delving into their social media profiles. Examine the timestamps when a person usually emails you, in addition to their word choice and general language. If someone emails you back consistently very late in the evening, then they might be a night owl.

It turns out that you can learn a lot about a person by studying their chronotype, or their distinct pattern of twenty-four-hour day and nighttime activity. Late-nighters may be introverted, anxious, and creative, while early-birds are more likely to be extroverted. Those who have trouble keeping to a regular sleep schedule are considered to be of a different chronotype; these people are more likely to be anxious and detail-oriented than the average sleeper and to experience high levels of stress.

A study conducted in 2010 by Beck and colleagues found that, contrary to expectations, people are more likely to present their authentic selves on social media platforms than their idealized ones. That is, people's online personas generally reflect their true selves. The findings of this study should be interpreted with caution, however, because the judgments people make are very general. Some aspects of character can be more difficult to gauge through online interactions. Some personality traits, like neuroticism, may be more concealed than others; extroversion and conscientiousness, for example, stand out more readily than the former.

Based on the photos they've posted, even profile pictures can give you an idea of where a person falls on the Big 5 scale. Research has found that people who score highly on openness to experience or neuroticism are more likely to have self-portraits in which they are the sole subject and their expression is neutral rather than happy. Pictures of happy, smiling people are more common among people who score highly on the personality traits of agreeableness, extroversion, and conscientiousness. Additionally, the latter two groups typically feature more vibrant colors and emotionally intense images.

It's also important to remember that knowing a person's idealized character can tell you a lot about who they really are. For instance, a person who likes to tell the world that they love traveling would most likely have a social media profile that is filled with their travel photos.

Let's put on that people-reader hat again, and this time, let's examine people through their online behavior:

Open an email or messaging app. Choose a conversation thread that you'd like to analyze. Carefully look at the timestamps. Do they respond to you quickly? Do they usually respond to you at night or at the start of the day? Based on the time they reply to you, what kind of person do you think they are?

Imagine that you are on a dating app. You matched with someone who seems really interesting. You had a really good conversation on the first three days. In fact, they replied quickly to your messages. However, in the following days, they just reply to you once a week. If someone has this online behavior, what kind of person do you think they are? Do you think they are interested in you?

_____

_____

_____

_____

_____

_____

_____

_____

_____

_____

_____

_____

_____

_____

_____

_____

_____

_____

Open a social media app (Facebook, Instagram, etc.). Choose a user profile that you would like to examine. Observe the content. What is their profile picture? What kinds of photos do they post? What are their word choices when it comes to their captions?

Based on your observations, what do you think the person is trying to communicate with their profile? What kind of personality do they have?

_____

_____

_____

_____

_____

_____

_____

_____

_____

_____

_____

_____

_____

_____

_____

_____

How can you better read someone's online behavior? Aside from timestamps and profile pages, what else will you look into so you can have enough information?

_____

_____

_____

_____

_____

_____

_____

_____

Reading People in the Workplace

In 2011, the journal _Social Influence_ published a paper that tried to find out if handshakes could help people make better judgments about each other. They asked the people who took the test to rate the personalities of five people they had just met. Half of the people did a handshake, and the other half did not. It turned out that the people who shook hands were better at judging how serious other people were than those who didn't. People in business who insist on meeting in person may have been on to something the whole time.

- Pay close attention to those few crucial moments if you want to get a read on someone after shaking their hand.
- A "dead fish" handshake can indicate a number of things, including low self-esteem, disinterest, or noncommitment.
- Sweaty palms can indicate anxiety, but not always—some people have naturally sweaty palms.
- Look to see who starts the shaking. Those who lean in close and squeeze too hard are attempting to exert control over the situation, possibly even to dominate the meeting in some way.
- When someone tries to angle their hand so that their palm is closer to the ground, they are symbolically attempting to "get on top" of the situation and command or control you.
- If done with a hug, watch to see who breaks from the shake first. Pulling away right away is a sign of unwillingness or hesitation, while lingering and shaking up and down for longer than is comfortable can

mean someone is trying to convince or reassure you.

- If someone gives you a delicate, limp hand to shake, almost like a queen giving her subject her hand to kiss, well, that says it all!
- A two-handed handshake, in which a second hand is placed over the first, is meant to show sincerity. However, it is more likely to be used by politicians or diplomats who want to look sincere, even though the effect can be a bit condescending.
- In general, a person is more outgoing and friendly if their handshake is open, warm, and easy.

Another way to assess your colleagues is to look at their social media. Don Kluemper, a researcher, found that people with social media accounts who seem conscientious, agreeable, and intellectually curious did better at their jobs.

But what if they post pictures of themselves always partying? Well, the general conclusion is that, well, context matters. Profiles were rated favorably when they showed people as having a wide range of interests, travel experience, plenty of friends, and interesting hobbies.

Now, let's apply these concepts to evaluate the people in your working environment:

Hop in a time machine and go back to your first day of work. On that day, you were probably introduced to your new colleagues. How did your colleagues welcome you? Did a handshake happen?

_____

_____

_____

_____

_____

_____

_____

_____

_____

_____

_____

_____

_____

Please describe a handshake you received, if any. Was it warm? Two-handed? Sweaty? Based on that handshake, what was your impression about your colleague?

_____
_____
_____
_____
_____
_____
_____
_____

If your colleague shakes your hand with another hand on top of it, what do you think is their personality?

_____
_____
_____
_____
_____
_____
_____
_____
_____
_____

Open one of your colleague's social media profiles. What do you see in their profile? What kind of content do they post? Does their profile match their personality in the office?

_____
_____
_____
_____
_____
_____
_____
_____

If someone's profile picture is an illustration instead of a real picture and the content they post are mostly memes and funny jokes, what could their personality be?

_____
_____
_____
_____
_____
_____
_____
_____

After learning all the indicators discussed in this section of the workbook (clothing, home and possessions, online behavior, and work behavior), how will you apply them in reading people? Which do you think is the easiest to observe? Which is the hardest?

_____

_____

_____

_____

_____

_____

_____

_____

Observation Can Be Active: How to Use Questions

In this section of the workbook, we will focus on what we can discover about others through directly asking them indirect questions. From there, we can learn much about people based on their answers. In many ways, it mirrors what we can understand about ourselves through the same process.

The focus is on people asking themselves simple, direct questions that, if answered correctly, might hint at truths just beyond our conscious knowledge. It is as simple as just asking, "What makes you happy?"

If you try to answer that question, it's easy to give a concrete answer. And this concrete answer can effortlessly reveal something about you. For instance, if you answer that traveling makes you happy, then it could give the other person a hint that you might be the outgoing type, or that you love nature.

In this next exercise, you will be required to talk to someone and ask them direct questions. After that, you will analyze the answers they have given and evaluate what kind of person they are.

DIRECT QUESTION 1: What was your greatest achievement and greatest failure?

Write their answer below. Observe their word choice and the focus of their answer. Does their answer fall in the category of career, family, or self? What do you think their answer says about them in general?

_____
_____
_____
_____
_____
_____
_____
_____
_____
_____
_____
_____
_____
_____
_____
_____
_____
_____
_____

If someone answers that their greatest achievement is to be able to sing in front of a huge crowd, what person do you think they are? What do they value the most?

_____
_____
_____
_____
_____
_____
_____
_____
_____
_____
_____
_____
_____
_____
_____
_____
_____
_____
_____
_____
_____
_____

DIRECT QUESTION 2: Which well-known figure or celebrity do you adore?

Write their answer below. What did they particularly like about the well-known figure? Do they admire them because of their status or personality? From their answer, what kind of person do you think they are?

_____
_____
_____
_____
_____
_____
_____
_____

If someone answers that they admire Adolf Hitler, what could this say about their personality?

_____
_____
_____
_____
_____
_____
_____
_____

DIRECT QUESTION 3: What's your favorite food?

Write their answer below. Are they into sweets? Or do they enjoy spicy foods? Based on their answer, what do you think is their personality?

_____
_____
_____
_____
_____
_____
_____
_____

If someone answers that their favorite food is anything that has veggies on it, what could this say about them?

_____
_____
_____
_____
_____
_____
_____
_____

DIRECT QUESTION 4: Ask someone a direct question that you made up on your own. In the space provided below, write that question and how you came up with it. Then, write down the response you received and what it revealed about the person you spoke with.

_____
_____
_____
_____
_____
_____
_____

How can you ask better direct questions in order to read someone? What factors should you consider when asking these types of questions?

_____
_____
_____
_____
_____
_____
_____

Indirect Questions, Direct Information

It is remarkable how much we can learn about someone's entire worldview or value system just by asking them a few basic questions. The previous task required you to ask clear questions in order to glean specific details.

In this final section of the chapter, you'll practice asking indirect questions and analyzing the responses you receive. These aren't simple yes or no questions; they're designed to provoke deep thought. So that we can begin to comprehend their actions and thoughts, the questions push individuals to reveal more about themselves.

For example, what if you asked someone where they got their news and which TV channel, set of publications, magazines, or pundits or hosts they liked best? It's a great example of an indirect question that can tell you a lot about how they think. It requires some guesswork and extrapolation, but at least there is a concrete piece of information to work with and many concrete connections to it.

In the next exercise, you will need another person's participation since you will be asking the indirect questions listed in the book:

INDIRECT QUESTION 1: What kind of prize would you work hardest for, and what punishment would you work hardest to avoid?

Analyze the other person's response and their emotion behind it. How did they feel about the question? What do you think motivates them? Are they motivated by pain or pleasure? What do they truly value?

_____

_____

_____

_____

_____

_____

_____

_____

_____

_____

_____

Interpret this answer: "I would work hard to get a million bucks, and I would work hard to avoid intimate relationships."

_____
_____
_____
_____
_____
_____
_____
_____
_____
_____
_____
_____
_____
_____
_____
_____
_____
_____
_____
_____
_____
_____

INDIRECT QUESTION 2: Where do you want to spend money, and where do you accept skimping on or skipping altogether?

What does the person's response say about how they view money? What priority or value were you able to identify based on their answer?

_____
_____
_____
_____
_____
_____
_____
_____
_____
_____
_____
_____
_____
_____
_____
_____
_____
_____
_____

Interpret this answer: "I would only spend my money on things that I know I need. I won't buy anything luxurious because they don't mean anything to me."

_____
_____
_____
_____
_____
_____
_____
_____
_____
_____
_____
_____
_____
_____
_____
_____
_____
_____
_____
_____
_____
_____

INDIRECT QUESTION 3: What is your most personally significant and meaningful achievement, and also your most meaningful disappointment or failure?

What does the person's response say about how they view themselves? Is it negative or positive? What self-identity do they have?

_____
_____
_____
_____
_____
_____
_____
_____
_____
_____
_____
_____
_____
_____
_____
_____
_____
_____

Interpret this answer: "My most personally significant and meaningful achievement is when I was able to be the top salesman in our company. My most meaningful failure is when I lost money because I got addicted to gambling."

_____
_____
_____
_____
_____
_____
_____
_____
_____
_____
_____
_____
_____
_____
_____
_____
_____
_____
_____
_____

INDIRECT QUESTION 4: What is effortless and what is always exhausting?

What does the person's response say about what they enjoy? Based on those activities they mentioned, what do they value?

_____
_____
_____
_____
_____
_____
_____
_____

Interpret this answer: "I find artistic activities effortless to do. I find it really exhausting to do household chores."

_____
_____
_____
_____
_____
_____
_____
_____

INDIRECT QUESTION 5: If you could design a character in a game, what traits would you emphasize and which would you ignore?

What does the person's response say about their ideal self? How is that ideal self different from their real self? What does this reveal about what they think is less important in the world?

_____
_____
_____
_____
_____
_____
_____
_____
_____
_____
_____
_____
_____
_____
_____
_____
_____
_____

Interpret this answer: "I would like to design a great mage. I would pump up their intelligence and dexterity so they can effortlessly cast spells. I will ignore agility and strength because they don't need those that much."

_____
_____
_____
_____
_____
_____
_____
_____
_____
_____
_____
_____
_____
_____
_____
_____
_____
_____
_____
_____

INDIRECT QUESTION 6: What charity would you donate millions to if you had to?

Reflect on the charity they have chosen. What sector in the world are they concerned about? What interests do they prioritize?

_____
_____
_____
_____
_____
_____
_____

Interpret this answer: "I would like to donate millions to an institution for mental health. I believe that it's important to take care of these institutions because mental health is a serious matter."

_____
_____
_____
_____
_____
_____
_____

INDIRECT QUESTION 7: What animal best describes you?

Did they choose a domesticated or dangerous animal? What do you think their animal choice says about their personality and what they value?

_____
_____
_____
_____
_____
_____
_____
_____

Interpret this answer: "I can describe myself best as a cat because I love to be alone. I also love to nap all day."

_____
_____
_____
_____
_____
_____
_____
_____

INDIRECT QUESTION 8: What's your favorite movie?

What did they personally like about the film? Do they identify with its character, or do they like the story in general? What is the narrative of that movie they are drawn to?

_____
_____
_____
_____
_____
_____
_____

Interpret this answer: "My favorite film of all time is _Inception_. I loved its concept and its exploration of the world of dreams. I am drawn to Leo DiCaprio's character because I think it's a cool job to invade people's dreams."

_____
_____
_____
_____
_____
_____
_____

INDIRECT QUESTION 9: What would you rescue from a fire in your home?

Will they save a family member or an inanimate possession? With their response, what do you think they value?

_____
_____
_____
_____
_____
_____
_____
_____

Interpret this answer: "I will save the oldest person in the house first because, unlike the young ones, they don't have the capacity to move around much."

_____
_____
_____
_____
_____
_____
_____
_____

INDIRECT QUESTION 10: What scares you the most?

Do they fear something that harms them physically or psychologically? What does their fear tell you about their principles? What does it tell you about their ability to handle suffering?

_____

_____

_____

_____

_____

_____

_____

_____

Interpret this answer: "I fear hanging bridges. I don't like them because of how unstable they make me feel. When I cross them, I feel like I'm going to fall anytime."

_____

_____

_____

_____

_____

_____

_____

How do you plan to improve your questioning skills and the way you interpret responses? In this chapter, what have you learned about questioning that will change your interactions from now on?

_____

_____

_____

_____

_____

_____

_____

_____

Takeaways

- When we want to understand other people, we can observe and think about a lot of things, but we usually don't have a lot of time to do so. "Thin-slicing" is the process of making accurate judgments based on small amounts of data. The accuracy of quick decisions based on thin-slices can be surprising. A good strategy is to go with your first instincts (intuition), but to back them up with more thought-out observations after the fact.

- Notice the words people use in their texts and emails, such as pronouns, active/passive voice, swearing, accent, word choice, and so on. Also pay attention to how emotionally charged someone's words are and if that amount is right for the situation. For example, using too much negativity in situations that seem harmless can be a sign of poor mental health or low self-esteem.

- You can learn a lot about a person by observing their living situation and personal belongings, much like you would by listening to and observing their body language and voice. Observe what someone has an abundance of and what is noticeably absent from the places they frequent. Personal items can be used to assert their identity, provide insight into their methods for managing their emotions, or serve as tangible proof of their past actions and tendencies.

- You can also infer people's personalities from their online actions, though exercise caution. Keep an eye out for the positive, neutral, and negative feelings conveyed by the pictures people post. Positive photo posters are more likely to be agreeable, extroverted, or conscientious, while neutral photo posters tend to score higher on openness and neuroticism.

- By asking the right questions, you can proactively glean a wealth of valuable insights. Asking hypothetical questions can break down people's defenses and elicit useful information from them quickly and openly. Your understanding of their innermost motivations, beliefs, and attitudes will improve greatly as a result of this.

Congratulations! You have reached the end of this workbook! Just a couple quick questions:

After answering all the exercises, do you now feel confident with your people-reading skills? Why or why not?

_____

_____

_____

_____

_____

_____

_____

Which of the methods do you still need to practice on? Which of them did you find the easiest to follow?

_____

_____

_____

_____

_____

_____

_____

_____

If someone is a great people-reader, what top five skills must they have?

1._____

_____

2._____

_____

3._____

_____

4._____

_____

5._____

_____

List five things that you learned about people-reading that you will surely apply in your future interactions.

1._____
_____
_____
_____
_____
_____
_____

2._____
_____
_____
_____
_____
_____
_____

3._____
_____
_____
_____
_____
_____
_____

4.

5.

Made in the USA
Las Vegas, NV
29 July 2023

75411864R00148